Edgar Rice Burroughs

Twayne's United States Authors Series

Kenneth Eble, Editor

University of Utah

TUSAS 499

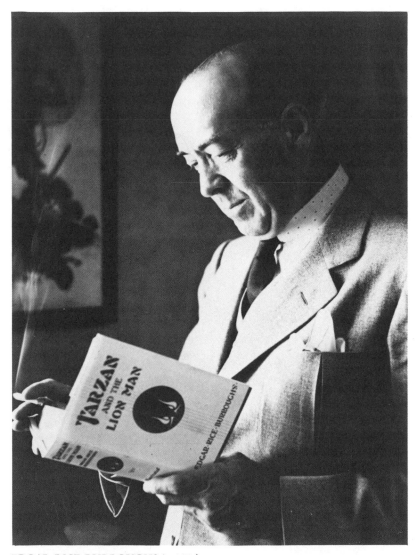

EDGAR RICE BURROUGHS in 1934
Photograph courtesy of
Edgar Rice Burroughs, Inc.

Edgar Rice Burroughs

By Erling B. Holtsmark

University of Iowa

Twayne Publishers • *Boston*

Edgar Rice Burroughs

Erling B. Holtsmark

Copyright © 1986 by G.K. Hall & Co.
All Rights Reserved
Published by Twayne Publishers
A Division of G.K. Hall & Co.
70 Lincoln Street
Boston, Massachusetts 02111

Copyediting supervised by Lewis DeSimone
Book production by Elizabeth Todesco
Book design by Barbara Anderson

Typeset in 11 pt. Garamond
by Modern Graphics, Inc., Weymouth, Massachusetts

Printed on permanent/durable acid-free paper
and bound in the United States of America

Library of Congress Cataloging in Publication Data

Holtsmark, Erling B., 1936–
  Edgar Rice Burroughs.

  (Twayne's United States authors series; TUSAS 499)
  Bibliography: p. 123
  Includes index.
  1. Burroughs, Edgar Rice, 1875–1950—Criticism and
interpretation.   2. Tarzan (Fictitious character)
  I. Title.   II. Series.
PS3503.U687Z69   1986   813'.52   85–27309
ISBN 0–8057–7459–9

給
媽
媽

For Dja Mung

Contents

About the Author

Erling B. Holtsmark received his B.A. degree in Greek from the University of California at Berkeley in 1959. In the academic year 1959–60 he was a Woodrow Wilson Fellow in classical philology at Harvard University, and in 1963 received his Ph.D. in classics from the University of California at Berkeley. In the fall of 1963 he began as an assistant professor in classics at the University of Iowa in Iowa City, where he now is professor and chair of the Department of Classics.

His teaching interests are the classical Greek and Latin languages, classical poetry, and Indo-European philology and myth. His research interests and publications range from Homeric poetry and Greek tragedy through Latin poetry up to modern reflexes of classical culture (including an earlier book on Burroughs entitled *Tarzan and Tradition: Classical Myth in Popular Literature* [1981]). He is currently at work on a book dealing with ancient myth and some of its implications for modern society.

Preface

With the exception of a period of some ten years in the late fifties and early sixties, enthusiasm for the works of Edgar Rice Burroughs has remained undiminished since his first publication, "Under the Moons of Mars" (later put out as the first book of the Martian series, *A Princess of Mars*), in *All-Story Magazine* in 1912. And that brief intermission was largely due to benign lethargy on the part of the Edgar Rice Burroughs Corporation in the matter of publishing or allowing publication of the founder's works.

Burroughs's commercial literary success is as remarkable as any found in the history of American publishing, and the legacy of financial good fortune continues for the author's heirs; over the years the literary creations (most notably Tarzan) have been profitably exploited in such other media as film, comics, radio, and television. The very name for his most famous hero, Tarzan, is now part of the English language, and appears in all modern dictionaries. *Webster's Ninth New Collegiate Dictionary* (1983), for example, also indicates that the word means "a well-built, agile and very strong man." Nobody knows how many of his books have been sold, but the number surely approaches or surpasses 100 million; the works have been translated into scores of languages, including the European languages, Arabic, and Urdu.

At the same time that Burroughs has enjoyed immense popular success, however, he has, until quite recently, been largely neglected or, at best, condescendingly brushed off by reviewers and those few academic critics who had deigned to discuss him. His was not, it was felt, serious literature, and hence not worthy of consideration. Yet, legions of readers, not all of whom have been uneducated, clearly have paid him great attention over the years. The books continue to sell briskly, especially so those dealing with Tarzan; and the Martian fantasies are acknowledged forerunners of the currently vast literature of so-called space operas, space westerns, or scientific romance.

In a book published three years ago, *Tarzan and Tradition: Classical Myth in Popular Literature,* I attempted to answer, at a fairly technical level, what it was about the early Tarzan novels that had made them endure, what it was about them, in other words, that had made them into minor classics of their own. Some readers were far from happy with my results there; others found them quite illuminating.

In the present study I do not aim either to win converts or create apostates. Here I expand the purview of that earlier study by ranging over the entire corpus of Burroughs's literary output; in consequence, the pages that follow are less rigorous and more given over to generalization of the sort to be expected in a less specialized study. Although I profess at the outset that I have been a devoted fan of Edgar Rice Burroughs (who more than any author awakened in me the realization that reading and literature were worthwhile enterprises) since I read the first Tarzan book at the age of twelve, I am not blind to the glaring weaknesses that he displays as author. Above all, I hope that what follows will be judged to be reasonably fair to both Burroughs and the distinguished tradition of which he is a significant modern representative. I do not hesitate to feature his blemishes any more than I am eager to demonstrate the resonatingly mythic universality of his fiction. Old fans of proven allegiance, like fresh recruits newly filled with wondrous admiration, will continue to read Burroughs no matter what arguments are advanced below. But it would be satisfying if this presentation induced some of those for whom all of Burroughs categorically represents the nadir of popular trash to subject their views to possible modification.

For that eventuality, I append my personal recommendation of Burroughs's ten best for a beginner's reading list: *A Princess of Mars, The Gods of Mars, The Master Mind of Mars, Tarzan of the Apes, The Return of Tarzan, Jungle Tales of Tarzan, The Land that Time Forgot, The Mucker, The War Chief,* and the quite atypical but delightful *I Am a Barbarian.*

Erling B. Holtsmark

University of Iowa

Acknowledgments

Many people have helped with this book, directly and indirectly.

It is appropriate to begin by thanking Professor Kenneth Eble, field editor, Twayne's United States Authors Series, for extending to me the invitation to write this book; he also deserves much credit for keen editorial criticism of the manuscript during its stages of growth. John LaBine, editor of the series, has been kind and courteous in helping to see my work through to a successful conclusion, and his comments have likewise done much to tighten rambling drafts. I also wish to express my thanks to Elizabeth B. Todesco for her splendid help during the production process of this book.

Two assistants have aided greatly in various aspects of research and editing, as well as proofing. I am happy to express public thanks to Lynn Leverenz and Callie Cardamone-Rawson for their industry at the final stages of preparation of this book. An earlier draft of parts of the manuscript was read and criticized by Birgit Holtsmark, to whom I am indebted also in many other ways. My secretary, Jane Davis, deserves thankful acknowledgment for covering the office front many times when I escaped to work on this book.

Marion T. Burroughs of Edgar Rice Burroughs, Inc., of Tarzana, California, has graciously permitted citations from material under copyright, and also provided the portrait of Edgar Rice Burroughs that appears as the frontispiece of this volume. She has been most generous and forthcoming in the matter of providing copyright notices as well as personal reminiscences of her father-in-law. I thank her for her kindness.

Finally, I wish to acknowledge the support and encouragement of my wife, Shu-Jiuan, a.k.a Dja Mung, to whom this book is dedicated with love and affection.

Copyright Notices

A Princess of Mars, copyright 1912 Frank A. Munsey Company; *Tarzan of the Apes,* copyright 1912 Frank A. Munsey Company; *The Gods of Mars,* copyright 1913 Frank A. Munsey Company; *The Return of Tarzan,* copyright 1913 Street and Smith; *Pellucidar,* copyright

Chronology

1875 Born in Chicago, Illinois on 1 September.

1881 Enters Brown School.

1887 Early interest in classical antiquity, especially mythology, as recorded in correspondence with older brother.

1888 Enters the Harvard School in Chicago.

1891 Interlude on the Burroughs ranch in Idaho; enters Phillips Academy in Andover, Massachusetts in fall.

1892 Enters Michigan Military Academy.

1895 Was graduated from same; fails entrance exams for West Point; becomes teacher at Michigan Military Academy.

1896 Enlists in army and is assigned to Troop B Seventh Cavalry in the Arizona Territory.

1897 Secures a discharge from army; begins work at father's firm, the American Battery Company.

1898 Returns to Idaho; opens stationery store in Pocatello.

1899 Travels to New York, returns to work at American Battery Company. Buys copy of *Descent of Man* by Charles Darwin.

1900 Marries grammar-school sweetheart Emma Hulbert in Chicago on 31 January.

1903 Travels with Emma to Idaho to join his brothers' mining company. First fiction written in this period (a fairy tale set in Idaho).

1904 In Salt Lake City, has job as railroad policeman; in Chicago, employed as construction worker, door-to-door book salesman, vendor of light bulbs, accountant.

1906 Tries to enlist in Chinese army.

1907 Has job at Sears, Roebuck, shows talent for managerial work.

1908 Daughter Joan born 12 January. Though successful at Sears, leaves security of this job to start his own business (which fails).

1909 Son Hulbert born 12 August. Turns down job offer from Sears, Roebuck.

1911 Begins writing *A Princess of Mars* in July, sells it before end of year. Begins *Tarzan of the Apes.*

1912 Metcalf of *All-Story* buys serial rights to *Tarzan of the Apes* for seven hundred dollars.

1913 Father dies 15 February, son John born 28 February. Travels to California (San Diego) with family for the winter.

1914 Returns to Chicago. *Tarzan of the Apes* sold as book to A. C. McClurg & Co.

1915 First sale to Hollywood; attempts script writing. Joins Author's League of America.

1916 Travels to Los Angeles. Difficulties with film producers. Plans to enlist for World War I.

1917 Appointed captain in reserves by state of Illinois.

1918 Movie release of *Tarzan of the Apes* and *The Romance of Tarzan.* Period of much patriotic, even chauvinistic journalism.

1919 Permanent move to California, where he buys estate (to be named Tarzana Ranch) in San Fernando Valley.

1922 Begins subdividing part of ranch to sell lots for houses.

1923 Incorporates self as Edgar Rice Burroughs, Inc.

1924 Plans to sell 120 acres of Tarzana ranch for country club.

1927 Joins anti-Prohibition group.

1929 First daily comic strip of Tarzan.

1930 Tarzana officially recognized as an independent post office.

1932 First Tarzan radio show.

1934 Divorces Emma Burroughs.

1935 Marries Florence Dearholt.

1940 Moves to Hawaii.

1941 Florence leaves him; columnist for the *Honolulu Advertiser.*

1942 Serves as war correspondent in South Pacific.

1944 Covers war as correspondent in Gilberts and Marshalls.

1949 Has serious heart attack.

1950 Dies on 19 March.

Chapter One

Edgar Rice Burroughs

Chicago, the heart of the American heartland, is perhaps as likely a birthplace as any for Edgar Rice Burroughs, the creator of so many fabled heroes in so many far-off lands and on so many distant planets. For there is a durable, recognizably American core in almost all the characters fashioned by the inventive imagination of this astonishingly prolific Midwestern writer.

Primary influences on the stories are his life-long interest in classical mythology and his studies of Greek and Latin in youth. Yet, ideals and attitudes of late nineteenth-century and early twentieth-century America are evident in many of the beliefs and outlooks of characters as different as the minor personality Danny "Gunner" Patrick in *Tarzan Triumphant,* who "hailed from Chicago" (26), and a central figure like John Carter of Mars.[1]

Despite the sense of period-piece that a reading of the major Burroughs works may occasionally engender, both the individuals and their tales are timeless, their roots pushing deep into the pre-American past. This grafting of a naive kind of nostalgic Americana onto mythic patterns of great antiquity perhaps helps to account for today's luxuriant flourishing of the Tarzan stories.

Childhood and Schooling

Edgar Rice Burroughs was born in Chicago on 1 September 1875 into a prosperous, upper middle-class home. His father, George Tyler Burroughs, had served in the Union army during the Civil War as a major, and had married Mary Evaline Zieger in Iowa City, Iowa on 23 February 1863. "After a wedding breakfast," Burroughs's mother observed in her memoirs, the newlyweds "left at once for Washington" (*ERB,* 774),[2] where George had received leave to get married. At the end of the war, the couple moved to Maine, where George began a furniture company.

In 1868 they and their two children, George Tyler, Jr. and Henry Studley, relocated to Chicago, and the father very quickly made a success of his new business venture, a distillery. Two more sons were born and survived, of whom Edgar Rice Burroughs was the youngest.[3] He appears to have been somewhat sickly as a child, and his parents, understandably concerned after the loss of other sons, seem to have doted on the youngest member of the family. The father was a stern man and something of a disciplinarian, and also proud of the financial prosperity and social success that his abilities in the world of business had won for the family. The mother exercised a tempering influence on his strictness toward the boys, but there is no doubt that he genuinely loved them and looked out for their interests. Family was important in the Burroughs household on Chicago's West Side, and everything points to a very secure and loving environment for the future creator of Tarzan.

Ed at first attended local public schools, but in the sixth grade was forced by his parents to transfer to a private school—and a girl's school at that! An outbreak of diphtheria prompted his parents to remove him from public school, and the only private place of instruction on the West Side was Mrs. K. S. Cooley's Maplehurst School for Girls. He did quite well there, especially in reading and geography.

Having finished grammar school, in the fall of 1888 Ed was enrolled in the Harvard School, a private institution located on Chicago's West Side. It was there that Ed was first introduced to the study of Latin, and all indications are that it was among his best subjects. For reasons not entirely clear he left the Harvard School in February of 1891, not yet a high school graduate. An interlude followed in which he was sent out to Idaho to work on the ranch that belonged to his older brothers George and Harry. His interest in animals in general and horses in particular took shape during this Western sojourn, and it was widely recognized that he had become an expert horseman who had a way with the animals. It may well be that this fondness of Burroughs for animals from a relatively young age manifests itself in his two most famous creations, Tarzan and John Carter of Mars. Both of these heroes have remarkable instincts and feelings for animals, and Tarzan is in some sense as much animal as he is man.

Burroughs by all accounts thoroughly enjoyed the rough-and-tumble of the cowboy's outdoor existence in Idaho, and was unhappy at the prospect of having to sit down on the school bench once more. His older brother Frank Coleman had attended Phillips Academy in Andover, Massachusetts, and the same fate was now plotted for sixteen-year-old Ed. He attended Phillips during 1891–92, where the course of study included liberal doses of Latin and Greek, along with English and mathematics.

It was apparent, however, that Ed's heart was not in his studies at Phillips, and his father was sent a formal request by the principal to withdraw his son from the school. Determined that Ed should finish at least high school, the elder Burroughs settled on a military school for his recalcitrant son; the boy was enrolled at Michigan Military Academy. There was heavy emphasis on discipline and physical conditioning, in addition to the normal academic subjects. Horsemanship was an integral part of the curriculum, and here Ed distinguished himself. Although he experienced unhappiness at the school's insistence on discipline and made several attempts to run away, he was graduated from the academy in 1895. Obviously not ecstatic while a student there, after graduation he nonetheless took on a position there as teacher (of geology). Restless as ever, however, the following spring (1896) he somewhat abruptly left his teaching position in order to pursue his latest fancy: a career as officer in the regular military.

The realization of this objective was not without its difficulties. He required the permission of his father, for he was under the legal age for enlistment. He needed further special consideration, this time from Washington, since he wished to be sent to a post not within the jurisdiction of the Detroit district, where he had signed up. At length he was assigned and posted to Fort Grant in the Arizona Territory in May of 1896, but before too long found that the realities on this outpost of civilization fell far short of the imagined adventures. Sickness (dysentary) aside, boredom and the futile tracking of elusive Apaches made his sojourn in the cavalry anything but exciting. In an impulsive manner that by now had begun to characterize his search for direction in life, he suddenly decided that he really should not be part of the military. By August he was sending desperate letters to his father to help him get mustered out. His father's influence was sufficient, if slow in coming, and in March of the following year (1897) Ed was discharged. Shuttling between work for his brothers in Idaho and his father in Chicago, the young man seemed incapable of forming any lasting attachment to plans and schemes for things to do. He tried art school and running a stationery store; he even toyed with the idea of enlisting in the army again, but was discouraged from doing so. Although he brought enormous enthusiasm to newly conceived projects, he appears to have had great difficulty sustaining it and carrying a project through to anything like a successful conclusion.

Marriage and Family

Certainly marriage to his childhood sweetheart, Emma Hulbert, in January of 1900, must have forced him to take a hard look at the direction of his life. Working for his father chafed at him, and he tossed about for ways to get away from under the older Burroughs's influence, no matter how benign and well intended it was. Thus, in 1903 he and Emma headed west for Idaho. The idea was that he would help his brothers in their gold dredging on the Snake River, but initial promises proved illusory, and the brothers' company soon floundered. Ed was lucky to get a temporary job as railroad policeman for the Oregon Short Line Railroad Company, located in Salt Lake City, Utah. He lasted only a few months, until October of 1904, at which point he resigned. He worked, in rapid succession, as timekeeper on a construction project, door-to-door book salesman, and as stenographer in the mail order department of Sears, Roebuck in Chicago; he had in the meantime also made some effort to find a commission in the Chinese army, going so far as to write the Chinese legation in Washington. The impression is quite unmistakenly that of a young man who has very little notion of what he wants to do with his life; when he got the Sears, Roebuck position in 1907 he was already thirty-one years old. Reports by his superiors indicate that he was a good and efficient worker, and promotions followed in order. This job appears to have been the first at which he demonstrated anything like sustained competence, and he might well have made a career of it. But his contrariness and fanciful approach to life soon got the better of him, and, as Porges puts it,

By 1908, Ed's record at Sears, Roebuck and his business efficiency and imagination had marked him in the eyes of the company executives as a man to be watched. A successful, stable career with steady advancement awaited him. Then, in a typically impulsive gesture, he abandoned his prospects and his future at Sears, Roebuck.

The previous failures to find anything permanent had left him undaunted. He decided to go into business for himself. (ERB, 101)

This move is all the more remarkable when viewed against the backdrop of his own advancing years and the recent arrival of his first child, Joan, in January of that year (1908).

The scheme this time was to enter into a partnership of sales and advertising, all on the strength of a correspondence course he had taken. The results were predictable and quickly realized. The added responsibility of a son, born in August of 1909, can only have made Ed all the more acutely aware of his need for some kind of steady employment, not to mention a stable career. Yet, when he received an unsolicited invitation from Sears, Roebuck to resume work for them as assistant office manager, he flatly turned them down. He was now involved in a project to write a course on salesmanship and then train the students by having them sell a variety of knickknacks door-to-door. The plan was that Ed and his partner would profit not only from selling their salesmanship course, but also from a cut of the items actually sold by the trainees. Although he was once more filled with unrealistic hopes of quick wealth, it soon became apparent that this latest venture was headed in the same direction as all the others—failure.

Writing Career

At this point in his life Burroughs seems to have reached the bottom. He was reduced to pawning his wife's jewelry in order to pay the household bills. While running a small enterprise devoted to the sale of pencil sharpeners, he began to write a fantastic tale about a man transported to the far-off planet of Mars, the princess he meets there, and the adventures that the two of them share. Starting in July of 1911, he completed the first half of the book in a month and mailed it off to *Argosy Magazine.* This story, "Under the Moons of Mars," was bought for four hundred dollars, and Burroughs was on his way. Writing would be his new career.

Initial success with the story of a distant world prompted him not to write another of this kind, but, in a perversely predictable deviation from proven success, to do a tale of medieval England entitled *The Outlaw of Torn.* Thomas Metcalf, the editor at *Argosy Magazine,* turned the story down, and Burroughs tossed about for another buyer. Initial success with his first story was not repeated with this second one, and it was only in August of 1913 that *New Story* magazine finally purchased serial rights to it for five hundred dollars. Persistence and perseverance in marketing his material had paid off, and throughout negotiations with various editors Burroughs had shown a sharpness about money and business that somehow had never surfaced in the countless failed ventures that up till this time had occupied him.

During the period between the selling of "Under the Moon of Mars" and *The Outlaw of Torn,* Burroughs had been busy on another project of fantastic dimensions, the story of the birth in Africa of a British child who comes to be raised by apes and in due course becomes their king. The child's name was Tarzan. Burroughs had first broached the idea in a letter to Metcalf dated 6 March 1912. Though encouraged by Metcalf, the problems he was encountering in trying to sell *The Outlaw of Torn* had assailed his burgeoning sense of confidence as a writer, and he seems to have had little hope during the writing of the first Tarzan book, *Tarzan of the Apes,* that he could sell it. Yet, the story did sell, and Metcalf sent him a check for seven hundred dollars. Burroughs was quick (and shrewd enough) to underscore that what Metcalf had bought was only serial rights to the story. It was published under his pseudonym (Norman Bean) and real name as the lead story in the October 1912 issue of *All-Story Magazine.*

During this period of initial if hard-won success as an author, Burroughs was working as manager for the service bureau of a business magazine. His job was to answer correspondence from businessmen in which they asked the advice of the magazine's expert staff of business consultants. The irony—and unethical nature—of the situation struck Burroughs, and he had harsh words for the venture. Despite the time required by these obligations, he found ample opportunity for writing and promoting his material, and a most productive period began. He learned what many writers have discovered: writing the stories is the easy part, and selling them is where the true perseverance must come into play. For even though he was by now (1913) well on his way, he still had numerous sharp exchanges with editors and publishing houses. To his great credit, Burroughs never lost faith in his own writing, whatever he may have said about it in belittling remarks to editors and others, but continued to stand up for legal ownership of his own property. He made no excuses about treating his writing as a product to be sold for the best possible price on the most favorable terms to himself.

At the same time it is clear that Burroughs did have certain ideas or notions that he promoted in his books. He was very much in the mainstream of the popular thinking of his day (and, needless to say, later generations of Americans also). The political frameworks that are constructed in his novels never seem so much to question or debate the value of existing institutions as they reflect a presumptive understanding about their essential validity. What a Tarzan or a John Carter imposed on foreign societies was a better and more just system than what had been in force, but it is worth noting that there is a very American assumption as well as presumption that "our" way is unquestionably desirable and therefore to be imposed. We may note that rarely if ever is there any debate about what kind of governance should be established—only about the means for inaugurating what is automatically assumed to be the only form possible: an American-style republican form of government. Both Tarzan and John Carter are agents of numerous such political transformations.

Dealings with Editors

In the fall of 1913 Burroughs took his wife and three children to California. The stated reason was concern for the children's health, which, Burroughs felt, was suffering from the harsh Chicago winters. They settled in Coronado, a community that bordered on San Diego proper. It was at this time that he got involved in newspaper syndication of his stories, dealing with the international Press Bureau. Both *The Return of Tarzan* and *The Cave Girl* were up for bids, and money coming in from the former was timely and welcome. Burroughs had no other means of support, and therefore threw himself into a vigorous schedule of writing and corresponding with editors. He began to enlarge the network of magazines with which he was willing to do business, no longer confining himself to Metcalf at *All-Story*. He was also involved with the editors of *Adventure* and *New Story Magazine,* both popular pulps of the day. Having begun the third Tarzan book *(The Beasts of Tarzan)* at the beginning of 1914 and having finished it in just over a month (7 January to 9 February), he played Sessions, editor for *New Story,* off against Metcalf of *All-Story* in order to get the highest possible price. Metcalf finally won the bidding with an offer of the then-princely sum of two thousand five hundred dollars, which was the most ever paid for a single story by the magazine.

But Burroughs's dealings with editors were far from over. He knew that his Tarzan stories were enormously popular, and thus felt justified in asking for payment rates that may well have been higher than the norm. The output of this period (late 1913 and early 1914) was truly enormous,[4] and it was clear to Burroughs that he could well afford to be selective about the editors and magazines with whom he worked.

By April of 1914 Burroughs had also engineered a contract for book publication of *Tarzan of the Apes,* and on 17 June of that year the first edition of the book was published by A. C. McClurg & Company. Financially secure and established as an author, he left California and returned to Chicago with his family, where he purchased a substantial home in Oak Park, a very comfortable suburb of the city.

The now familiar intensity in writing continued. Burroughs turned out sequels to series already started, including the fourth Martian novel *(Thuvia, Maid of Mars)* and *The Cave Man,* the latter a sequel to *The Cave Girl,* published in the previous year. Submission and publication of *The Cave Man* illustrates a general principle about Burroughs the literary businessman. He became embroiled in something of a controversy about word counts with Bob Davis, his editor at the Munsey Company, publishers of *All-Story Cavalier.* This was not uncommon for Burroughs. Porges discusses correspondence on the subject, and gives a vivid picture of Burroughs's "almost obsessive fear of being underpaid" *(ERB,* 208).

During this period Burroughs was busy with Hollywood, the start of a long and unhappy relationship. The style and narrative verve that characterized his novels and worked so effectively to the public's satisfaction were, however, not translatable to script writing. Although he tried his hand at a number of scripts, the results seem to have been less than felicitous. Despite initial resistance from Hollywood to Tarzan, when Burroughs did succeed in selling the movie rights and saw the resultant product, his disappointment was keen. To his sorrow, the author learned that once the rights had been sold, he had no control over what was done with the property.

Patriotism and Politics

When the First World War broke out in early 1917, Burroughs was eager to involve himself. Ever since the days at the military academy in Michigan and the stint in the United States Army in Arizona, it is clear that Burroughs was fascinated by military life and the military in general. One of his most famous heroes, John Carter of Barsoom, was after all mustered out of the Confederate army before he made the great journey to Mars, and Tarzan was an active participant against the Germans in the Great War (*Tarzan the Untamed*) and the Japanese in the Second World War (*Tarzan and the Foreign Legion*).

In 1917, however, Burroughs was already forty-one, a bit old to sign up for the troops. He therefore tried to get into action as a war correspondent, a tack that did not, ironically, pay off until some twenty-five years later when, in Hawaii, he became a correspondent for the Pacific theater in the Second World War. He was urged by the commandant of the Michigan Military Academy to join the reserves, and he promptly filed an application. He returned to Chicago, and soon thereafter the state of Illinois accepted him as a captain in the reserves.

Burroughs proved to be a strong patriot, almost fanatical on the subject of what was and was not genuine patriotism, and here manifested some of those qualities of militarism that had become so prominent in the persona of John Carter. He seems to have been quite severe with those his own age who were not actively engaged in some form of support for the prosecution of the war against Germany. During this period the question of translations of his Tarzan novels into German had been broached by a publisher, but Burroughs was quite unwilling to pursue the matter. Indeed, he was vociferously anti-German, as is obvious from his books. The Germans are depicted in highly derogatory stereotypes as incarnations of evil and cruelty, and Burroughs seems to have been reflecting contemporary notions in the popular mind about Germans.

Financial Success

Although he had returned to Chicago rather abruptly, he did not stay for long. His sense of duty fulfilled by joining the reserves, he made the decision to leave the Midwest for good. The lure of California was simply too strong. Thus, in February of 1919 he arrived once more in Los Angeles, and now looked about for a suitable home for Emma and the three children. He settled on an estate of some 540 acres owned by Harrison Gray Otis, founder of the *Los*

Angeles Times, and located in the San Fernando Valley. It was named the Tarzana Ranch, and both horses and livestock were kept on it. This was the property that, beginning in 1923, was subdivided into lots for homes and was subsequently incorporated as the city of Tarzana, which still exists under its own postmark (granted in December of 1930).

The writing and negotiating about works already completed continued apace, including some complicated and lucrative movie contracts. Although the latter involved sums handsome for the times, Burroughs was never happy with the cinematic side of his growing empire. Perhaps it was the loss of ultimate control over his own products that rankled, together with inability to exercise any meaningful control over other projects in which he got involved.

Be that as it may, it is quite clear that by the early twenties his enormous literary productivity, supported by a no-nonsense approach to the commercial side of writing, had put him well along the path to becoming a rich man. In 1921, for example, his income from the strictly literary properties totaled an astonishing $98,238.28 (*ERB,* 340).

The twenties were years of increasing financial security, continued writing and business dealings, and the growth of the three children into adulthood. Although the latter did not have their father's literary talent or ambition, the second son had inherited the father's ability with a sketch pen and ended up doing a number of illustrations for the books in the thirties and forties. The books themselves were written in spite of Burroughs's expressed weariness with both Tarzan and the Martian series. Particularly in the books about the apeman one is able to discern a diminution in the vitality of the plots as a result of the inevitable repetitions in themes and sequences. How many times was it possible to tell the tale of a fallen man redeemed by the love of a virtuous woman, of yet another civilization found in some remote jungle enclave, of a tyrant-priest ruling his people despotically before being overthrown by Tarzan's efforts, of the hero suffering amnesia due to a blow to the head, of the confusion engendered by doubles, or of Tarzan's rescue by the last-minute arrival of his son Jack, the loyal Waziri, or some other helper? Burroughs clearly asked himself this question on a number of occasions, but he seems to have become something of an indentured servant to the very popularity of his creations. Pleading lack of interest and physical exhaustion, he was nonetheless prevailed upon by editors not to cease writing about his hugely successful characters. No doubt some positive stimulus was exercised on Burroughs by the fact that Tarzan had now been widely translated. In fact, by 1925 Tarzan could be read in at least seventeen different languages, and the royalties from the foreign sales were considerable. In this connection it is of interest to observe that although so many of the most villainous monsters in the Tarzan books were either Russian or German, in both countries Tarzan was a phenomenal success and enjoyed huge sales. It is noteworthy that the first Martian novel was written in 1911, and the last one thirty years later about 1940; the spread between the first and last Tarzan novel was even greater, covering some thirty-five years from 1912 to about 1947. However much he may have grown weary of his own literary children, he continued to tend and nurture them almost to the end of his life in 1950.

During the thirties Tarzan was also a radio program (as it was to become, briefly, a television series in the sixties), and some of the merchandising potential of Burroughs's various creations was exploited on different fronts. It was also in the thirties that the illustrated versions of Tarzan came into its own, continuing up to the present day, appearing in this country and many foreign ones as well. Such superb illustrators as Hal Foster (creator, subsequently, of Prince Valiant), Burne Hogarth, and Russ Manning all contributed to the distinguished iconographic tradition of Tarzan, who was among the very first cartoon heroes. Burroughs appears to have enjoyed the visual interpretations of Tarzan much more than he did the cinematic ones, and owned a number of original sheets of comic art. In this connection it should be noted that illustrations for books and dust jackets have enjoyed a long history, each generation reflecting its own version of what the hero should be visually.

Personal Problems

During this active and even hectic period of the twenties and early thirties both Burroughs and his wife succumbed to various illnesses, some clearly organic in nature and others with a more vague or diffuse etiology. It must be recalled that Burroughs was now approaching sixty years of age, and it is perhaps not surprising that things, even indeterminate things, should begin to go wrong. This is not to say that Burroughs lived or acted like an old man, for he was still fond of horseback riding, as well as golf and tennis, and at the age of fifty-eight learned how to fly. Although his wife did develop a severe drinking problem, and Burroughs appears from time to time to have gone on the wagon, he was a strong opponent of Prohibition. He resented the governmental intrusion on private enjoyment, and quite correctly appreciated the horrendous consequences of the Volstead Act for the growth of organized crime in America. At the same time more than one character in the novels (including Tarzan) have objections to or end up in trouble as a result of alcohol, and it seems safe to infer that Burroughs had little use for excessive consumption of liquor. As his wife's increasing lack of control of her drinking became obvious, the relationship between them grew more strained. These difficulties came to a head in early 1934, when, at the age of fifty-eight, he left home; divorce followed, being formally granted on 6 December of that year. On 4 April of the following year (1935), Burroughs married Florence Dearholt, herself divorced and a friend of the family, who was about half as old as Burroughs at the time. The newlyweds honeymooned in Hawaii, and subsequently divided their time between Los Angeles and Palm Springs.

From all accounts, the marriage between Burroughs and Florence was initially a happy one. Her children, about six and four at the time, took readily to their step-father, and he to them. Porges notes that he endeared himself to them in part by telling them the same exciting adventures he had recounted to his own three children a generation earlier *(ERB,* 613ff.).

In spite of the fact that Burroughs was far from poor, his life style was apparently too extravagant and expensive, and in the late thirties he appears to have worried a great deal about how to finance his daily existence in the wealthy world of Los Angeles celebrities. His solution to this nettlesome concern was the decision to move to Hawaii, where, he thought, he would be able to carry on in a less elegant and costly fashion. In April of 1940 he and Florence sailed with the children for the islands, and here Burroughs settled into a regular nine-to-four schedule of writing; in September of that year he had finished a John Carter story, the last one in the Martian series *(John Carter of Mars).*

Hawaii hardly proved an idyll, however. Various difficulties (which seem to have been primarily financial in origin) began to drain the marriage of its earlier joy, and Burroughs took to drinking heavily, going so far as to keep a stock hidden under his bed. He appears to have become more and more dependent on Florence for the everyday details of his life, and friends who saw the couple at this time were not sanguine about the future of the relationship. In March of 1941 she left him, sailing back to the mainland with her children. Burroughs went on the wagon for two months, and when he fell off again he continued to have problems with the alcohol; Florence filed for divorce. Burroughs's physical ailments, no doubt exacerbated by the drinking, caused him great discomfort and pain, and he was in and out of hospitals in the fall of 1941, leaving instructions about his funeral with Ralph Rothmund, his secretary of many years. Despite the pessimism about his health or his preoccupation with death he was to live for another nine years.

Final Decade

Such problems as he did have were eclipsed by the momentous events of 7 December 1941, to which Burroughs, as chance would have it, was personal eyewitness. Along with his son Hulbert, who was visiting at the time, he heeded a general call for able-bodied men to come to reporting stations. Ironically, the sixty-six-year-old Burroughs, who had not been able to volunteer for World War I, became a sentry on a wharf that very night. Later Burroughs's writing ability was put to good use, for he acquired a position as columnist whose primary task was to promote civilian morale. Entitled "Laugh It Off," this column first appeared in the issue of 13 December of the *Honolulu Advertiser,* and contained material designed to be both frivolous and serious, commenting on civilian efforts to help the military and guard against further Japanese attacks.

After a couple of months the column was discontinued, and Burroughs became involved in the so-called Businessmen's Military Training Corps, where he functioned as a drill master. As always full of ideas and opinions, he proposed ways and means for defending the islands, among which measures was the unhappy one of evacuating all Nisei to the mainland. Although admitting that not all Japanese living in Hawaii were pro-Japan, he clearly revealed his "susceptibility to the blind panic and prejudice of the period" *(ERB,* 630). This initial attitude toward the Nisei did in the course of the war undergo an almost complete reversal, and in a September 1944 article he comes strongly to the defense of the Japanese-Americans

who had served honorably on America's side against Japan. Toward
the end of 1942, after serious effort on his own part and that of
friends, he was accredited as a war correspondent by United Press.
In December 1942 he flew out on a military transport, and spent
the next week covering activities in New Caledonia and Australia.
He returned to Hawaii aboard a destroyer, and conceived a great
dislike for the navy, which would not accept his credentials as a
correspondent. It must be noted that his disdain was not strictly
due to a kind of naval blockade of his dispatches, but the service's
stinginess about alcohol for nonnaval personnel. In March of 1944
Burroughs once more flew out to the Pacific theater, covering the
Gilberts and Marshalls. It was in the course of this trip that he
formulated the specifics for the twenty-second Tarzan novel, *Tarzan
and the Foreign Legion,* set in Sumatra.

Toward the end of the war Burroughs's wife, Emma, the mother
of his children, died of a stroke. Her drinking, which had been the
triggering cause for their divorce, had gotten completely out of
hand, and before her death she had been under the care of various
doctors, all to no avail. Burroughs returned to the mainland, and
at the same time managed to see the families of all his children as
well as Florence and her two children. While in California, Burroughs himself came under a doctor's care, in his case for a hernia
operation. After a sojourn of almost three months, he returned to
the islands in early February of 1945. He now took up, once more,
the column he had begun at the start of the war and shortly discontinued, "Laugh It Off." Of interest is the fact that in an April
(1945) column Burroughs gave expansive praise to the new Dem-
ocratic president, Harry Truman; Burroughs can hardly be seen as
a liberal in his political thinking, yet he obviously admired Truman's
candor and no-nonsense approach. The strong populist streak in
Burroughs clearly meshed with similar sentiments in the president.

At the time of his visit to California, Burroughs was sixty-nine
years old. To the consternation of his sons, he had met and formed
a serious attachment to a woman, and now contemplated marrying
her. The plan was deflected by a sudden invitation from the United
States Navy to sail on a fleet oiler as war correspondent in the
Pacific. He wrote several pieces for United Press about the activities
of such a ship in the late Pacific campaigns. He spent approximately
two months in this assignment. Toward the very end of the war
and into the fall of 1945 Burroughs began to be seriously bothered

by attacks of angina pectoris, and was confined to bed for over a month. In late October he flew back to California and civilian life, and before the year was out had purchased a house for himself in Encino.

Although Burroughs had been writing at a frantic pace just prior to the outbreak of the war, the paper shortage of the early forties had blocked publication of any Burroughs works for some four years. Nor did Burroughs do much writing after the war was over. He was tired by now, for the exertions of his travels in the Pacific under trying circumstances, at an age (late sixties) when other men were content to sit back, had taken their toll. His health was not good, for in addition to the angina he also had problems with arteriosclerosis. Although he tried to get back into the rhythm of writing, he seems no longer to have had it in him. While fiction-writing may have been reduced to a bare minimum, Burroughs's long-standing habit of carrying on extensive correspondence showed little sign of flagging. Some of his letter-friends were fans with whom he had been in touch for more than a generation.

During the late forties his health continued to deteriorate. He was now in his mid-seventies, and was quite conscious of what was happening to him. The despondence he felt at the inevitability of aging and deteriorating physically is not hard to understand. A serious heart attack in December of 1949 signaled the beginning of his demise, and on 19 March 1950 he died suddenly. He was cremated, and his ashes placed beneath a tree in Tarzana. Never a believer in organized religion, Burroughs did, a short time before the end, give some indication of what he thought or hoped might follow: "If there is a hereafter, I want to travel through space to visit other planets" *(ERB,* 699).

And it is to one of these planets, Mars, and the world that Burroughs created there that we now turn in the following chapter.

Chapter Two
John Carter, Warlord of Mars

Mars is where it all started for Burroughs.

It is safe to say that next to the Tarzan novels, the eleven volumes of the Martian cycle have been of greatest significance in shaping and securing Burroughs's reputation as a writer of popular fiction. Among the seventy-odd tales that he penned during his writing career of forty years, none can compete in sheer spectacle or inventiveness with what we find in these often clever stories of an exhausted planet. Even the Tarzan books, predicated as they are on a most willing suspension of disbelief by the reader, do not scale the imaginative heights of the Martian material. Tarzan is a profounder character, to be sure, than John Carter, but his stories do not contain the biting and at times Swiftian overtones that so often resonate throughout this dying world of Barsoom (Mars). For it is on the planet Barsoom, remotely distant from his earth in both time and space, that Burroughs gave most dazzling rein to his sense of amusement and bemusement at the world that he himself inhabited.

Typical Plot

Broadly defined, the typical plot of the Martian novels unfolds a hero's journey to a distant place in search of a woman whom he either loves or thinks he loves. She has been abducted by a lecherous strongman eager both for the woman's body (the famous "fate worse than death,"[1] e.g., *John Carter of Mars,* 143) and her value as a bargaining counter in his bid for political or military power. Often the hero misinterprets the woman's aloofness as prompted by his own unworthiness or lack of understanding of females. Encounters with peoples or races morally as well as physically monstrous are a staple feature in the search. One or more rulers are met, and these usually are villains, often lording over a cowed and fearful populace. The hero somehow becomes the catalyst for revolution and the replacement of the evil ruler, usually by a younger man who earlier had escaped or been taken captive from his homeland and imprisoned in a far country, where the hero meets him as a fellow-slave or prisoner. The woman, who is at least ostensibly the central focus of the hero's quest, is likely to fend admirably for her virtue and work actively for her own escape and return until the hero reaches her. She may, however, prove to be a weak and vacillating vamp, like the beautiful but treacherous Sanoma Tora of *A Fighting Man of Mars*. At times the true "princess" is discovered only in the end of the book.

Sizeable chunks of ethnographic and cultural data are stuffed into the narrative cracks on the road of the hero's quest, and numerous secondary routes peel off onto intriguing byways of Martian lore and civilization. Of special interest in this connection are such standard items as the descriptions of Martian architecture and histories of the numerous dead cities dotting a desolate landscape; discussions of the planet's population policies and her sophisticated achievements (including what are today called computers)[2] in the physical and biological sciences (especially the pharmacological and neuro-surgical specialties of medicine); analyses of the manifold expressions of religion (largely equated with superstition) and political organization; reflections on the physical environment of Mars as well as the intellectual and linguistic characteristics of her many strange peoples; and a host of obiter dicta on subjects ranging from the mundane (e.g., Martian foods and eating habits) and merely interesting (e.g., Martian breeding practices or assassins' guilds) to the extraordinary (e.g., the highly developed ability of most Martians to read the thoughts of others) and indeed marvelous (e.g., normal life spans of up to a thousand years).

These seemingly incidental features form from the very first novel so integral a part of the narrative flow that the reader almost imperceptibly dons the many assumptions, material and ideological, on which Mars, like any society or civilization, is predicated. It is among other things precisely the creation of a world that Burroughs has undertaken in the Martian series. Relatively little such background is in evidence in the Venus of Carson Napier, for example, and even in the richly variegated tapestry of the Tarzan books there is not the sense of cohesiveness and continuity that informs Burroughs's Mars—a world that he first fashioned in 1911 and continued to work in all its static timelessness for another thirty years.

Informing Design: *Katabasis*

The orienting grid along whose multiple axes the individual features of the books are plotted is the *katabasis*, or death and descent into the underworld. Here lies the core myth that informs the entire Martian corpus on both gross and detailed levels. There is no disputing the pervasiveness and prominence of *katabasis* in the myths of classical antiquity.[3] Here its two most prominent exemplars are Odysseus's trip down into Hades's place in book 11 of the Homeric *Odyssey,* and Aeneas's trip to the realms of Dis in book 6 of Vergil's *Aeneid,* both heroes well known to Burroughs. The mesmerizing power that this fabled journey has exercised on the western literary imagination throughout the millenia is harnessed by Burroughs in the opening of his first novel, *A Princess of Mars.*

The tone is indelibly set, most persistently through the use of vocabulary. It will be recalled that the hero is holed up in a cavern in the Arizona hills after his partner has been killed by a band of renegade Apaches, and that he repeatedly underscores the fact of his own death and resurrection, not to mention the observation that his dead body had been preserved intact while he himself was mysteriously transported to far Mars.[4] The planet itself is repeatedly characterized as a dying world, and indeed the book concludes on a note of cosmic catastrophe in the seeming inevitability of the entire planet's demise as the result of a failure in the Atmosphere Factory. Carter's falling into unconsciousness on Mars just before waking up once more in the Arizona cave, is a thinly veiled image for death, and one that Burroughs was to embroider time and time again into the textures of his tales. The words "death," "die," "dying," "dead," etc. are evident on almost every page of the book— a search of just the first two chapters shows nineteen occurrences in ten pages of text. And there are of course many concepts and synonymous expressions for death worked into the narrative, such as unconsiousness, mortality, narrow defiles, tunnels, subterranean passageways, descents into pits, caves, and Stygian darkness.

The paradigm. The hero is on a journey, usually at night or a time of darkness, and in a forest or grove of some kind. The purpose of his trip is to gather wealth (which may be in the form of tangible assets such as gold, or of information and knowledge) or to rescue a friend or woman, frequently his wife. Some kind of physical boundary (mountains, forests, rivers, other topographically

delimiting features) marks the end of the real world and the beginning of the other, that is, world of death. The entryway is normally
a cave, grotto, or chasm, perhaps a narrow passage or defile through
a mountain, and at some stage a body of water (usually a river) or
marshland must be crossed. Any place beneath the earth, such as a
tunnel, pit, or subterranean chamber, is a typical form of displace-
ment for the underworld. In the case of a watery boundary, a boat
or raft provides the physical means for passage; a guide or companion
of some sort often accompanies the hero. Conditions are imposed
on the hero (e.g., don't look back, eat nothing found here), as are
various forms of testing. These probings of his worth may be manifested as either physical or intellectual and spiritual. The hero is
not afraid to admit his fearfulness at times during his journey to
the beyond, especially as he encounters various monsters, spirits,
demons, and other worldly denizens, most of whom are hostile. He
does often meet with a wisdom-figure, however, who explains things
about the hero himself or his situation in the real world. Finally,
the return is made, but it is often fraught with special difficulty
and obstacles. The hero brings back wealth, whether physical or
spiritual (or both), to the real world.

An example: Carter's death and rebirth.   Consider the details
of the start of the first novel: Carter's dying away from a hopeless
situation on earth only to be reborn on Mars as shaper of his own
fortunes.

When we meet the hero he is at his nadir. He has a fistful of
worthless money and a commission in a nonexistent army, and has
just spent a year of extreme hardship in the Arizona wilds pros-
pecting for gold. At last a strike is found, and his partner sets off
for civilization to bring back much-needed equipment and men to
work the claim. But Carter is unhappy witness to his friend's death
at the hands of a gang of marauding Apaches, and, though dis-
claiming any credit for heroism, in traditionally heroic fashion sets
out to recover the corpse of his slain partner from the violating
enemy. In turn pursued by the Indians, he inadvertently eludes
them by turning into a defile and coming upon the entrance to a
great cave. Here is forced to admit that his companion is indeed
dead, and abandons the attempt to revive him. Crawling into the
cave, the hero tries to fend off his drowsiness, recognizing that sleep
at this point can mean only death at the hands of his pursuers.

When he wakes up, the Indians have begun to encircle him inside

the cave, but suddenly flee in precipitous fright, leaving him alone
with the corpse of his friend in the strange cave that harbors some
mysterious power. Enduring the "silence of the dead" (*A Princess of
Mars*, 18) among the "black shadows" of the cave "until possibly
midnight," he heard "a faint rustling as of dead leaves" and is quite
suddenly liberated from his own body. The entire description is a
classic formulation of the start of the heroic *katabasis* that leads to
rebirth. As Carter himself remarks:

And the moonlight flooded the cave, and there before me lay my own
body as it had been lying all these hours, with the eyes staring toward
the open ledge and the hands resting limply upon the ground. I looked
first at my lifeless clay there upon the floor of the cave and then down at
myself in utter bewilderment; for there I lay clothed, and yet here I stood
but naked as at the minute of my birth. (19)

The concluding simile is surely not without point in this neatly
orchestrated launching of the hero on his descent into the underworld
of the chthonic cave. In the case of this hero, of course, the descent
is the miraculous transition "through extreme cold and utter darkness" (20) to the brilliant sunlight of Martian midday, where the
heat "was rather intense upon my naked body." This motif of rebirth, so central to the narrative design of the *katabasis,* is underscored in several ways. First are the repeated references to the hero's
nakedness (five times in pages 19 through 25). Next is the observation that, because the lesser gravity of Mars makes his normal
walking more like leaping, he must learn to move by "reverting to
first principles in locomotion, creeping," much as a child learns to
walk. And, finally, his very first experience on Mars, even before
the initial encounter with Martians, is the discovery that he has
landed in a hatchery where the young of one of the races of Mars
are just emerging from their eggs; Carter describes the process of
their birth in detail, as well as the new-born creatures themselves.
This striking juxtaposition of death (including his own) against birth
(including his own, as it were) at the beginning of the first of the
Martian novels would seem to be an unmistakable index to the
author's thematic plan for his hero. Nor, as we shall see, do subsequent developments disappoint this created expectation. The series
begins, then, on a highly traditional note, fully identifying the tale
to follow as heroic epic in the most conventional sense of that phrase.

Characters

The hero: warrior and lover. The story of John Carter and his sojourn on the far planet of Mars is a tale of escape and adventure, a narrative of an omnipotent hero who overcomes all obstacles and makes his own luck, bending even the most adverse of circumstances to his own advantage and eventual triumph. It is a tale of powerful romance and shimmering fantasy; it features a hero who is at all times a master of his destiny, never quite ready to give up or in. While he still lives, the hero remarks on numerous occasions, he refuses to believe that there is nothing more he can do to better the odds for survival and success in whatever disastrous situation he may for the moment find himself. As hero, John Carter of Virginia is eternal optimist and dedicated doer of deeds.

Born of the imagination of Burroughs, who in 1911 might well have felt that he was up against the intractable demands of personal circumstances, the hero is easily seen as a projection, a kind of wish-fulfillment fantasy of his creator.[5] And though this may be the case, it hardly explains the powerful hold that the Martian cycle has exercised on the popular imagination for the last seventy years—a hold that continues in full strength today. Somehow Burroughs, who surely was not alone in his own or later days in having to face the practical demands of daily existence, was able to articulate a heroic vision compounded as much from his own sense of personal inadequacy as from his keen sense of the classical myths on which he drew so strongly in shaping this fiction. It is the unremitting flux of life and love in alternation with hostility and death that captivates us. Burroughs's Carter reveals to our daydreams a romantic vista of the possibilities for what we would like to believe might be and could take place. The unspoken but constant assumption is that of a dying away from the here-and-now with its impinging demands to a rebirth into a distant world, a fantasy land where all is possible, and power over self and others attainable.

Carter was conceived and developed in an age of relative innocence, the period just prior to the First World War, when America had begun to see itself as a world power whose ideals should be actively promoted as worthy of emulation abroad. Although Carter is not so much interested in the democratization of Mars as he is in pursuing the quite personal ends of demonstrating his prowess as warrior, he *does* get involved in the planet's politics, and he *does* have a say in the internal developments of some Martian cities. But this is incidental to his primary objectives, almost a matter of serendipity.

All true heroes are also lovers, and hence the amatory element in the form of the captive Dejah Thoris makes its first appearance early in *A Princess of Mars*. And Burroughs, with a very fine sense of linguistic antithesis as well as the larger frame of reference of birth and death in which he has placed his hero, describes Carter's falling in love as follows (my italics): "And so, in silence, we walked the surface of a *dying* world, but in the breast of one of us at least had been *born* that which is ever *oldest*, yet ever *new*" (*A Princess of Mars*, 73).

Like all of Burroughs's heroes, Carter does not have much experience with women, and this unfamiliarity translates itself into a kind of bumbling shyness and naïveté in their presence. It is of course quite conventional that the hero should, among other things, be educated about his sexuality, and we find this aspect of the hero's development prominent in all the traditional heroes of "high" literature, beginning with a Gilgamesh, Odysseus, or Aeneas. And not only Carter, but other secondary heroes throughout the eleven novels are cast in a similar mold: initial awkwardness at the feeling of love, rejection real or imagined, and final understanding of how to handle this important part of maturation. For we find this same approach to amatory relationships in the case of Carter's son Carthoris and his princess, Thuvia of Ptarth (*Thuvia, Maid of Mars*), of Gahan of Gathol and Tara (*The Chessmen of Mars*), of Vor Daj and Janai (*Synthetic Men of Mars*), of Tan Hadron and Tavia (*A Fighting Man of Mars*), and of Ulysses Paxton and Valla Dia (*The Mastermind of Mars*), to mention some of the more prominent examples.

Carter (and his many heroic doubles in the series) unquestionably trace their ancestry as amatory heroes back to the great heros of antiquity in conceptual terms, but as concrete exemplars of the type (i.e., erotic hero) they are very much anchored in the mainstream of modern popular fiction. Indeed, in this very matter of the hero's entanglements in affairs of the heart, one sees clearly the extent to which Burroughs cloaks contemporary expectations in ancient dress. For the nobility and sheer chivalry of the Burroughs lover link him in some ways more persuasively with the late medieval tradition of courtly love that eventuates in the popular romance of self-sacrificing love winning its true reward than with the ancient prototypes.

Superficially, then, a Carter as erotic protagonist has the visible trappings of his traditional counterpart but little of the interior exploration of conflicting loyalties and responsibilities that so typically reveals itself in the classical hero. Quite the opposite seems to be the case, for Burroughs's heroes think nothing of placing an entire kingdom at risk in the pursuit of a single woman who is the beloved. They are more a Trojan Paris than a Roman Aeneas in their insouciant disregard for societal consequences of personal passions. True, everything turns out fine in the end, but the tenor is very much that of simple male (and female) wish-fulfillment of the kind that is alleged never to sweeten the pages of "serious" literature.

This eroticizing of the hero places him squarely in the world of comedy—and comedy in literature is not necessarily a question merely of guffaws, but rather of an attitude and an outlook on the world. Burroughs was something of a prankster and had a keen sense of humor *(ERB,* 28–31, 40–44, and passim), and this spirit finds ample documentation throughout many of the novels in the Martian as well as other series; but the matter is more complex than simple laughs. In the world of comedy, be it Aristophanic drama, Plautine farce, Shakespearean romance, or a Bugs Bunny cartoon, the forces of good and evil are always in a precarious balance. Only in the final scene does this teetering walk on the razor's edge of uncertainty end with a resolution that favors the side of good and harmony (frequently, as in the Martian novels, emblematically represented by a wedding). Burroughs's Martian universe is stretched taut by the eternal conflict between love and war, two actions and attitudes that variously manifest themselves as birth and death, creation and destruction, tenderness and cruelty, and many similar polarities. In the elite suburb of high-brow we speak of a novel's "tensions" and in the vulgar ghetto of popular literature we talk of the "cliff-hanger," but the literary mapping is identical even if imposed on a variant topography. The central characterization of the hero as a lover and warrior, traditional enough in its own right,[6] speaks precisely to the informing template of these competing forces at work in the Martian tales. These tensions tend, however, in the Burroughs corpus to be largely externalized as the protagonists' actions rather than internalized as thought, speculation, or questioning, and hence comes the inevitable sense of characters largely lacking depth and genuine personalities.[7]

Now, the warrior-hero may be a fighter for the Greeks of Agamemnon, the Trojans of Hektor, the Christianity of the pope, the empire of Queen Victoria, or any other specific group or set of beliefs, but he must display this general feature. And Burroughs's warrior-hero, cut to an utterly traditional pattern, is wrapped in cloth of specifically American weave. His war, in short, is the war of liberation, of opposition to tyranny, of the good guys against the bad, and this ideological dress on a hero conceived along strictly classical lines marks him as a more complex personality than might at first seem to be the case: he has become an easily recognizable vehicle for conveying a particular point of view about popular American values (and in no age are a culture's values wholly consistent with its realities) in the early part of the twentieth century. Militarism, a sense of manifest destiny, the idea that America knows best for the world (especially the more alien, non-European world)—these were part and parcel of official American policy in administrations as different as those of Teddy Roosevelt and Woodrow Wilson, and these notions are encapsulated in Burroughs's hero.

We may certainly criticize the author for easy acquiescence in society's values instead of questioning them. But one can, in fairness, hardly fault him for not taking a Dreiser-like stand on the issue of war while he clearly does so on a number of other now (but not in the early 1900s) fashionable concerns such as ecology, the population explosion and, significantly, the dangers as well as blessings of high technology.

The villains: scientists and despots.   The Martian villains keep busy getting in the way of the hero and complicating his life, and some are considerably more interesting than the hero himself. Although the possibilities for discussion are legion, perhaps no villain is more intriguing than the fabulous scientist-surgeon Ras Thavas, the Master Mind of Mars.

It is only in propaganda that villainy is absolute, uncomplicated by any ameliorating considerations. Even so repulsive a monster as the unspeakable Ghron, Jed of Ghasta, in *A Fighting Man of Mars,* is marginally exonerated by the narrator-hero, Tan Hadron of Hastor, as being utterly mad, maniacal and diseased,[8] and a Ras Thavas, relatively benign by comparison, attains to a kind of heroic stature of monstrousness. Certainly the novel's protagonist, Vad Varo (a.k.a. Ulysses Paxton), has mixed feelings about Ras Thavas, for the latter is as much a benefactor of the hero as he is his nemesis. This villain is interesting precisely because he is an ambiguous villain, not evil incarnate but a complex mixture of altruism and sadism, scientific genius and moral idiocy . . . but let Burroughs introduce him:

He was guilty of the most diabolical cruelties and the basest of crimes; yet in the next moment he might perform a deed that if duplicated upon Earth would have raised him to the highest pinnacle of man's esteem. Though I know that I am safe in saying that he was never prompted to a cruel or criminal act by base motives, neither was he ever urged to a humanitarian one by high motives. . . . I know that he would not operate for money alone and I have seen him devote days to the study of a scientific problem. . . . (21)

The strokes with which the author here depicts Ras Thavas color the reader's subliminal perception of the man as a subject in whom the external appearance of an ordered control is mere translucent glaze highlighting an underlying reality of chaotic contradictoriness of mind and action.

In *The Mastermind of Mars,* where we first meet Ras Thavas, we have a classic story on the pattern of the *katabasis.* The hero, Paxton, with his evocative first name of Ulysses, has at the opening of the book been severely wounded in France during World War I. His legs have been blown off between the knees and hips. He prays for death, and suddenly stands on two good legs dispassionately viewing the mutilated remains of his own body. At the next moment he is transported into space. In short, dead on the battlefield of war, he is miraculously reborn and transplanted to Mars, the planet named for the Roman god of war.

He finds himself in the city of Morbus,[9] where he encounters a very old man (Ras Thavas) who has shriveled away to almost nothing. The latter brings Ulysses into his laboratory, a great hall filled with corpses and parts of corpses, which resembles a mortuary, and proceeds to embalm for storage the body of an individual Paxton had been fighting. Once "descended" into this warehouse of the dead, Ulysses begins the arduous process of learning transplant surgery from Ras, and soon is himself capable of quite literally raising the living from the dead. The constant push-pull throughout the novel between death and rebirth is the informing design that enables us to evaluate not only the heroicness of the book's Odyssean hero but also the monstrousness of its fascinating monster.

Ras's technical skills are startling in their perfection. Martian science in general and its medicine in particular have been developed to a much higher degree than on earth, but even in this heady atmosphere of technological resourcefulness the abilities of Ras Thavas as transplant surgeon stagger the imagination. And, as is made evident in the subsequent *(Synthetic Men of Mars)*, where he is featured, his astonishing if misguided experiments in what today is known as genetic engineering qualify him as a typical "mad scientist."

The prototypical mad scientist is of course Dr. Frankenstein, the eponymous creator of the monster Frankenstein. That story, published in 1818 by Mary Shelley, is a product of deep romanticism, and its variations have continued to fascinate. There can be little question that Burroughs was familar with the story,[10] probably through reading and surely from the famous Boris Karloff film of 1932.

The particular twist that this Frankenstein theme takes in *Synthetic Men of Mars* (written in 1938) entwines a kind of high genetic tech with a militaristic adventurism. Ras Thavas had been driven out of his established estate in the Toonolian marshes at the end of *The Mastermind of Mars,* and had conceived a scheme to recapture the ceded land by creating an army of synthetic soldiers.

But—and here is Burroughs's point—there is always the possibility of a technological boomerang effect: the shaper of what he believes to be a boon for himself or mankind finds his creation somehow getting out of control and effecting totally unexpected (and usually most undesirable) results. Ras had planned to continue his experiments after regaining his territory with the help of the artificial soldiers: "Some day I shall create the perfect man, and a new race of supermen will inhabit Barsoom—beautiful, intelligent, deathless" *(Synthetic Men of Mars,* 34). We must note that such a statement in the context of events in Europe in the late 1930s will have been suggestive of one of the more repellent aspects of the so-called philosophy of the Nazi *Uebermensch*. But two unforeseen circumstances have arisen that force Ras to reconsider. First, even the soldiers, though not created for beauty, are misshaped grotesques, at least half of them to such an extent that they must be destroyed as useless for warfare; and, second, the politicians have got their collective finger in the genetic vats, and they now have their own notion of what this potentially exciting technology can do for their more immediate ends.

Ras Thavas as villain is thus an imaginative amalgam of classical monster-magician types and the romantic fascination with exploring the limits of man's darker inventive impulses. He is the most interesting of the villains in the corpus of the Martian tales, and is one of the few to redeem himself and be converted to a "good guy." The seeds of his better nature assert themselves at the end, and Mars (in particular Helium) is the better off for it. It is precisely this ethical ambiguity about the man and his works that makes him into a compelling character, remembered long after the scores of more rigorously defined villains and monsters peppered throughout the novels have lost their tang and ceased to excite the reader's imagination.

Most of the hero's opponents are more straight-forward villains, endowed with an uncompromising evil that is clearly reflected in exterior ugliness. Many of these characters are, like the infamous Ghron mentioned above, despotic rulers of their little kingdoms or enclaves. In the first novel, again, a typical monster is introduced, and the pattern according to which he is described sets a theme on which endless variations are run throughout the Martian corpus. The jeddak (supreme ruler) of the greenmen into whose hands Carter falls is Tal Hajus. This evil potentate of Thark is hated by many of his subjects, including Tars Tarkas, the greenman who becomes a close friend of Carter. Tal Hajus is, like many monsters, a creature of voracious sexual appetite, and Burroughs, with his flair for incongruous and even grotesque pairings in these matters, presents him as sadistically enamoured of Dejah Thoris: first she is to be "his," and then she will be subjected to excruciating physical torment so that he can "watch that beautiful face writhe in the agony of torture" (*A Princess of Mars*, 97). As one might expect, Tal Hajus is himself no lovely sight to behold, for his exterior appearance is an accurate reflection of the unmitigated malevolence that drives him:

the most hideous beast I had ever put my eyes upon. He had all the cold, hard, cruel, terrible features of the green warriors, but accentuated and debased by the animal passions to which he had given himself over for many years. There was not a mark of dignity or pride upon his bestial countenance, while his enormous bulk spread itself out upon the platform where he squatted like some huge devil fish, his six limbs accentuating the similarity in a horrible and startling manner. (96)

Burroughs quite clearly was fond of this particular amatory configuration (the bestial or beastlike monster carnally passionate for a defenseless woman), for its unmistakable contour is outlined time and time again—and not just in the Martian novels. It seems to have been for Burroughs one of the two or three major defining endowments of villainy, and in this he quite clearly follows precedent set thousands of years ago: monsters have an uncontainable appetite for food and sex, and are greedy beyond measure for temporal power. Tal Hajus is a conventionally impeccable if ultimately uninteresting monster, utterly without the complicating ambiguities that make a Ras Thavas so intriguing a villain.

And there are many, many others of the same ilk. Among them are the brutal Salensus Oll of Okar (*The Warlord of Mars,* 136), the implacable Nutus of Dusar (*Thuvia, Maid of Mars,* 125–26), the lecherous Ul Vas, jeddak of the Tarids (*Swords of Mars,* 144–45), the synthetic Pew Mogel, who has built his own monster of destruction, Joog (*John Carter of Mars,* 28–35), and the Zorian father-son pair of tyrannical monsters Zu Tith and Multis Par (*John Carter of Mars,* 92).

A final observation on villains and monsters is in order. For there is a further extension of the concept "monster" or "villain" that, like a thin but continuous strand of concern, threads its way in and out of the larger weave of the novels. This is an abstraction: religious superstition (*not* religion as such) shamelessly exploited by an elite few to hold the planet's people in thrall. For of all the evil and incarnate monstrousness that populates Mars, none is more pervasive and more pervasively undermining to its civilization than the monstrous sham that religion, perverted into a blind and unreasoning superstition, has become. This shady hustle is more than adumbrated in the first novel, and is fully exposed in the second one, *The Gods of Mars;* here its nefarious effects are blunted by the rationalistic iconoclasm of the protagonist, who in this context is surely more than a destructive warlord with a single-minded heroism that wants only to do battle with sword and fist.

The heroines: romantic independents. Like the men, the women on Mars run the gamut from beautiful and mighty, like Dejah Thoris, to ugly and powerless, like Sola, and, like the male protagonists, they are quite predictable. The essence of the kind of literature that Burroughs was writing entails repetition of the narrow detail as well as the encompassing theme, and such iteration can easily tend to obviate the possibility for interesting variety. Especially in the case of heroic literature, with its roots in folklore and myth, can this reliance on the familiar and the conventional become a deadening liability. This tends, by and large, to be the case for the heroines that are met on Barsoom.

The woman who is central to the series and against whom all other females are measured is Dejah Thoris, daughter of Mors Kajak the jed of Lesser Helium and granddaughter of Tardos Mors, jeddak of Helium. Both her father and grandfather are eponymous of death, [11] which makes her into the typical princess of folktale whose father (here "doubled" as both father and grandfather) is a death-demon the hero must overcome in order to win the daughter. She is a woman of great personal courage and resolve, and she has a strong sense of pride in herself and her position within Martian society.

As the first of a long line of Burroughs heroines, she is something of a trend-setter. Two other famous heroines, Jane Porter, who becomes the wife of Tarzan, and Meriem, who marries Tarzan's son Korak, are both fashioned on the same model. Perhaps the central characterizing feature of these women is their inner toughness and their determination not to be overwhelmed by circumstances. The latter show up in the form of lurid villains with specifically erotic designs. The threat of violence, sexual or merely physical, is a common fixed scene in which the woman is featured. Although physical violence is in fact perpetrated on some of them, the accomplishment (as opposed to the threat) of a specifically sexual attack is quite rare. [12]

This eroticising of relationships and the implicit assumption about the power of sex and sexuality in political or dynastic contexts are common literary territory for any shaper of heroic tales. The powerfully sexual personality of an Odysseus or an Aeneas can hardly be denied, nor is it far from the surface in endless medieval epics, despite the ostensible and often ostentatious piety of their nominally Christian heroes. The point is that what may at first sight appear on Burroughs's part to be a slick appeal to prurience is in fact an intimate concomitant of precisely the kind of literature that he is composing.

Another Martian heroine, less central to the entire series than Dejah Thoris but equally typical, is Thuvia[13] of Ptarth. Two suits are pressed upon her, that of Astok, Prince of Dusar, and that of Carthoris, Prince of Helium and son of John Carter and Dejah Thoris. Astok's physical eagerness is deflected by the intervention of Carthoris, whose own yearning for the women, though not manifested in a similar violence, is nonetheless as firmly rebuffed. For Thuvia of Ptarth is promised in dynastic marriage to Kulan Tith, jeddak of Kaol.

This archetypal scene of conflicting triangular relationships locates the heroine at the apex so to speak, and soon enough she is abducted. Not unlike Helen of Troy, Thuvia of Ptarth becomes the potential cause for war between Ptarth and Helium, for it is believed in Ptarth that Carthoris was her abductor. Carthoris will disprove the suspicion by rescuing the girl from Astok, the actual forager, and sets off in pursuit. The rest of the book, at least from the point of view of Thuvia, is a replay of this basic theme: the woman, desired by a villain, is rescued by (and also in her turn helps) the hero. For like the other heroines, Thuvia is a driving force behind the adventures to which the hero subjects himself; without her Carthoris would have had no reason to set out on his quest. This fact should not obscure the independent characterization of the women and the fact that they all star in their own versions of the quest, the battle, the descent into hell, and the re-emergence into "this" world and the full integration of the self: the initial disequilibrium of abduction is dispelled by that most traditional of harmonizers in the comic mode, marriage.

Concluding Remarks

The Martian novels are not systematically concerned with extrapolating from contemporary trends to possible future developments. There is, however, a kind of desultory prognosticating about then unknown but now common technological applications of scientific discovery, like computers, avionics, transplant surgery, telecommunications, and laser technology, and there is plenty of discussion of what are now fashionable concerns, such as the depletion of natural resources, overpopulation, and general ecological imbalance. Yet, although these dangers appear to constitute important underlying assumptions about Burroughs's Mars, except at the end of the first novel and the beginning of the second they have very little to do with the stories. It is more a background against which the fantastic adventures of the hero are set than a central problem to be explored and pushed to the farthest possible limits of speculation. As with so much in Burroughs, the implications of created expectations are all too often neglected in favor of pure action.

Despite the emphasis on fast action and inventive plots, however, speculation is not totally lacking from these books. One might well wish that Burroughs had given in to it more often. A striking example is the social problem attendant on organ storage, the acquisition of young and beautiful bodies for parts-purchase by wealthy old people who desire to be rejuvenated (see especially *The Mastermind of Mars*). Long before Robin Cook's successful novel *Coma*, Burroughs had addressed in some detail the question of what such a trade might lead to, and his conclusions anticipate those of Cook. And Burroughs's thoughts on the dangers of a purely intellectualized and scientific approach to the living of life are well illustrated in the horrors that scientific experimentation can bring about (as with the "vats of life" in *Synthetic Men of Mars*). Burroughs liked to think of himself as a forward-looking individual with an enlightenmentlike view of rational progress and scientific discovery, but he was much too sensible not to be fully aware that science can be a two-edged sword, and a very sharp one at that. Thus, it is not that Burroughs was incapable of following through on possible outcomes of speculative trends he had set in motion, but seems simply not to have been interested in doing so. Action and complex, if often improbable, plots were his real metier in these tales.

Setting up phenomenological conundrums like those generated by the phantom bowmen of Lothar in *Thuvia, Maid of Mars*, however, Burroughs does move beyond mere story-telling. He seems to be evincing interest in the proposition that there are severe limits on a purely mentalist or intellectualist position about the nature of reality. In a similar vein, in one of the most amusing (yet with an underlying seriousness) and laugh-provoking sequences in the entire Martian series, a like position is suggested by the encounter with the strange kaldanes in *The Chessmen of Mars*. They are pure head, ugly beyond belief but highly intelligent, and they need a rykor, or body, in order to move about with ease—faute de mieux, they can perambulate on six short spidery legs. The bodies, beautiful creations, are dull and listless things without the directing force of a kaldane plugged into their cervical receptacles. The unemotional intellectualism of these peculiar Bantoomians reminds one character (Tara) of the snobbery she had often encountered among some scholars of self-styled superiority in Helium (58). Like them, the kaldanes seem to think that any holistic approach to the living of life is a waste, for only the brain and its pursuits matter. The hero of the book, Gahan of Gathol, refutes the argument, insisting on a balanced outlook that does not give exclusive attention to the demands of the intellect, but fair billing also to the passions of the body. In a remarkable discussion emphasizing the necessity for moderation and balance, Gahan would seem to be articulating views that Burroughs held dear about the need for harmony in the living of one's intellectual and physical life (88–90).

Thus, although incidental discussion and considered reflection on social, scientific, and quasiphilosophical subjects are dispersed among the novels, there is no genuinely systematic or consistent inquiry into Martian institutions or practices. There is much description but little real analysis, a great deal of action but no attempt at elucidating teleology, colorful character types but few realized personalities. To be sure, Burroughs was admittedly writing popular entertainment, and one should perhaps not look for anything else. But in reading these books one is constantly chagrined at the author's prolific waste of possibilities—possibilities that, seized upon, need not have detracted from the narrative rush. There is an unfortunate sense of so many good scenes and situations simply thrown away in order to get on with the next rescue or the next descent into a cave or Stygian tunnel. For all the flowing readability of the stories, what keeps them from sustaining literary curiosity is their failure to generate any ontological interest either in themselves or beyond.

Chapter Three
Tarzan: Literary Background and Themes

The centrality of Tarzan to Burroughs's stature as a writer of popular American fiction can hardly be disputed. Although the twenty-four novels in which the apeman is featured constitute approximately a third of the author's output, they are disproportionately responsible for his reputation and popularity. The Martian series has captivated its share of devotees, but these novels, along with the minor works, have not equaled the impact of the Tarzan tales.[1]

It is an unfortunate irony that the vehicle primarily responsible for the enormous popularity of Tarzan, the films, is at the same time notoriously misrepresentative of the Tarzan that emerges from a reading of the novels. It is a further irony that Burroughs, for all his justified discontent with the butchering to which Hollywood subjected his characters, seems to have adopted some of the mannerisms of the celluloid copies in his characterization of the hero in novels of the later thirties and early forties. Most notable in this connection is Tarzan's lapsing into monosyllabic or pidginlike English of the sort immortalized by Johnny Weismuller's portrayal of Tarzan. It is quite clear from the Tarzan of the early and middle novels that he was highly articulate and indeed a phenomenal linguist.

The overarching plot of these stories stands on the solid foundation of a quest. In this regard it is clear that the stories are drawn after the image of the classical hero-tales, all of which entail a questing of one sort or another. As we noted in the last chapter, heroic quests tend to fall into three broadly definable categories: the quest for 1) wealth, 2) wisdom, and 3) another human being. These groupings are themselves further definable, so that the quest for wealth, for example, may realize itself as the hunt for animals (witness the many formulaic scenes of Tarzan's ranging for food), or the pursuit of treasure (as in *Tarzan and the Jewels of Opar* or *Tarzan, Lord of the Jungle*).

Before we consider the quest in specific books, it will do well to sketch the contours of a typical Tarzan tale. The peace of the jungle is disturbed by the arrival of Europeans, invariably bent upon some wild scheme of enrichment involving lost civilizations, elephant poaching, slave trading, or some combination of these. A white woman is a member of the expedition, and may be an innocent or a schemer; she is the subject of countless abductions by crazed Europeans, greedy Arabs, or lust-smitten apes, only to be repeatedly rescued by her European wooer, faithful Waziri, a friendly animal, Tarzan himself, or her own (often hitherto untested) toughness.

Enmeshed in this network of prurient treasure-hunting are the strands of personal heroism and cowardice, moral degradation and personal redemption, the flowering of love, the conflicting claims of civilization and savagery, and the guiding authority that the apeman exercises in the far reaches of his vast realms. It is Tarzan the hero who imposes, by physical exertion or cunning presence of mind, an order on the jungle world of animals, natives, and foreign intruders.

The Classical Background

The character of Tarzan as he emerges from the novels is by no means that of the one-dimensional and at times moronic creature fashioned by Hollywood, but a complex literary figure. Both textual evidence and information now available about Burroughs's life from the massive biography by Porges may be adduced as evidence for locating the literary Tarzan in the richly traditional milieu of classical epic and myth. Burroughs did not invent Tarzan out of whole cloth, nor did he steal the idea of Tarzan.

It has nonetheless been alleged (*ERB,* 129) that Burroughs simply stole Rudyard Kipling's Mowgli, or at least the idea behind Mowgli (an abandoned child is adopted by wild animals and reared among them to adulthood), and made the East Indian wolf-boy over into the British ape-child. One might with equal validity assert that he stole the character from Homer; that he merely copied patterns available from any text of classical mythology; that he usurped the personality developed for his hero by the popular American writer Owen Wister in his famous novel *The Virginian,* published in May of 1902[2] or that he filched people and plots from any one of perhaps dozens of other possible candidates, both ancient and modern, who had written hero-stories before he did.

Ancient authors who leap to mind are (in addition to Homer) Livy, Plutarch, Ovid, and Vergil. Burroughs had read these authors, some in the original Greek and Latin.[3] Among the moderns, in addition to Kipling and Wister, Burroughs certainly was familiar also with Charles Dickens, Thomas Macauley, Jack London, Zane Grey, Anthony Hope, and the countless writers of pulps in the late nineteenth and early twentieth centuries. A strong case has been made by Richard A. Lupoff[4] that H. Rider Haggard was a major influence on Burroughs, especially in the latter's development of the character La of Opar from Haggard's *She.* But the Homeric Circe or Calypso and Ovid's portraits of passionate women are equally likely sources, and we do know that Burroughs was well acquainted with the stories in the Homeric epic as well as those told by Ovid in his *Metamorphoses.* In short, talk about literary robbery too readily turns glib, and, furthermore, the undeniable reality of literary borrowing and adaptation from earlier writers is an inextricable part of all literary activity from the earliest epics of Greece to the latest popular romances.

In *Tarzan and the Golden Lion* there is a pointed reference to Tarzan linking up with the divinities of ancient mythology: "Not as the muscles of the blacksmith or the professional strong man were the muscles of Tarzan of the Apes, but rather as those of Mercury or Apollo, so symmetrically balanced were their proportions, suggesting only the great strength that lay in them" (42).

Quite similar in intent is the passage in *Tarzan and the City of Gold* in which we read about Tarzan as follows: "Tall, magnificently proportioned, muscled more like Apollo than like Hercules, garbed only in a narrow G string of lion skin with a lion's tail depending before and behind, he presented a splendid figure of primitive manhood that suggested more, perhaps, the demigod of the forest than it did man" (10). Somewhat tongue-in-cheek, moreover, in this passage Burroughs allows Tarzan to be dressed in the traditional lion's skin that Hercules wore, and of course underscores the typically Apollonian (with Odyssean overtones) feature of Tarzan's weaponry, the bow and arrow: "Such a bow was this that no ordinary mortal might bend it" (11).

Burroughs's familiarity with the languages and literatures of classical antiquity is evident from a number of indices internal to the texts. Consider, for example, Tarzan's characterization of himself to a credulous challenger of his right to be abroad in the city of the

Athneans: " 'I am Daimon,' replied Tarzan. . . . To Daimon they attributed all unexplained deaths, especially those that occurred at night" (*Tarzan the Magnificent,* 160). Only someone familiar with classical Greek would use the term Daimon (a direct transliteration of the Greek word for any kind of personal spirit or minor divinity) in this fashion. And in *Tarzan and the Foreign Legion* the pilot Jerry Lucas quotes an English translation from the opening of Vergil's *Aeneid* in order to underscore his understanding of Corrie van der Meer's implacable hatred for the Japanese: " 'Haughty Juno's unrelenting hate,' quoted Jerry" (78).[5] It is clear, furthermore, that the allusion is carefully thought out by the author, for a few lines earlier a motivation for the citation of Vergil is established by Corrie's manner of killing a Japanese soldier:

He [Jerry] saw her stand above her victim like an avenging *goddess.* Three times she drove the bayonet into the breast of the soldier. The American watched girl's [*sic*] face. It was not distorted by rage or hate or vengeance. It was illumined by a *divine* light of exaltation. [my italics]

In the same novel the professional Bubonovitch tosses off a reference to Thermopylae, and at a later point quotes a Latin translation from Plutarch: *"Et tu, Brute"* (147).

One of the novels (*Tarzan and the Lost Empire*) involves the discovery in Africa of a lost civilization that still maintains the ways of ancient Rome, and the young classical[6] scholar Erich von Harben, first encountering their language, "recognized the tongue as a hybrid of Latin and Bantu root words, though the inflections appeared to be uniformly those of the Latin language" (37). At a later point, after he has become, however unwillingly, associated with the court of the Emperor of the East, von Harben lives the lovely fantasy that any classicist might well entertain with relish:

And often in the library he discovered only unadulterated pleasure in his work, and thoughts of escape were driven from his mind by discoveries of such gems as original Latin translations of Homer and the hitherto unknown manuscripts of Vergil, Cicero and Caesar—manuscripts that dated from the days of the young republic and on down the centuries to include one of the early satires of Juvenal. (85)

In *Tarzan at the Earth's Core* the quester Jason[7] at one point becomes involved with a bewitching young lady, Jana of Zoram, and in dignified self-mockery describes his bootless pursuit of her: " 'Odysseus never met a more potent Circe. Nor one half so lovely,' he added, as he regretfully recalled the charms of the little barbarian" (108).

It is of course not necessary that the reader be aware of Homer's *Odyssey* in order to make sense of this passage. Just as the reference to Troy and the Trojan War in *Jungle Tales of Tarzan* (11) sort out the underlying tensions of that passage, however, so both the author and the hero (Jason) in the current passage inform the reader of a kind of grid that is to be laid across the present tale to enable us to see it not only as just any hero-tale, but as one involving great journeys into fairylands, encounters with traditional monsters (e.g., the Horibs in *Tarzan at the Earth's Core),* and the unceasing quest to return home (which here is the outer world beyond Pellucidar). In short, we are to see the story as part of a lengthy tradition beginning in ancient epic, where, it might be noted in passing, Odysseus's ship and Jason's Argo are the typological equivalents of the great dirigible 0-220 that takes Jason, Tarzan, and the others into Pellucidar. One might note, finally, the unmistakable imprint of the Greek romances[8] on the elaborately constructed plot-antecedents at the beginning of *Tarzan Triumphant.*

The Modern Background

Although the entire Tarzan construct is a very precise working-out of mythical and classical themes, it is equally clear that the author has drawn not only on classical antiquity for his creation of the apeman; he is also very much anchored in his own age and his own peculiarly American heritage. This latter is most intriguingly manifest in the Amerindian element that has gone into Tarzan's makeup. Burroughs had himself been part of the Apache wars in the Arizona Territory in the late 1890s. He seems to have conceived a strong respect and empathy with the Indians, which figured prominently in his two later novels, *The War Chief* (published in 1927) and *Apache Devil* (published in 1933). Nor should one dismiss the importance of the incorporation in the composite Tarzan of such traits as were popularly attributed to Indians: stamina, resourcefulness, intimate knowledge of animals and nature, tricksterism, and much else.

Some auctorial editorializing in the books suggests other interests

Burroughs had that may well also have contributed to his development of the Tarzan story. A passage from *Tarzan and the Golden Lion* indicates that Burroughs had done some reading about Africa in connection with the Stanley expedition, probably for general background information on the locales in which his characters were placed (110). It is at any rate clear from Porges's biography that Burroughs had done research at the beginning of his writing career, in particular to get an overall sense of the world in which he was to place his new creation, Tarzan.[9]

Nor was Burroughs beyond doing some research for later novels, both those dealing with Tarzan and other characters. Thus, for example, he contacted the Chicago Field Museum for information on the life and customs of the Apaches (*ERB*, 421). In connection with *Tarzan at the Earth's Core* Burroughs did considerable study on the characteristics of dirigibles in order to lend authenticity to his depictions of the ship 0-220 (*ERB*, 471). And the author's preface to *Tarzan and the Foreign Legion* indicates that not only had he queried various individuals familiar with the general ambience of Sumatra, but had also consulted the Netherlands Information Bureau in New York, as well as the Honolulu Public Library (the latter without success).

For the more literary or plot-conditioned variables of his stories Burroughs was as much a prisoner of the literary scene of his own and preceding ages as the author of any other period. For example, Burroughs never had any qualms about admitting that he had read Kipling, though he claimed that he preferred the man's poetry to his prose. And when asked about the possible relationship between his Tarzan and Kipling's Mowgli, he commented as follows:[10]

To Mr. Kipling as to Mr. Haggard I owe a debt of gratitude for having stimulated my youthful imagination and this I gladly acknowledge, but Mr. Wells I have never read and consequently his stories of Mars could not have influenced me in any way.

The Mowgli theme is several years older than Mr. Kipling. It is older than books. Doubtless it is older than the first attempts of man to evolve a written language. It is found in the myths and legends of many peoples, the most notable, possibly, being the legend of Romulus and Remus, which stimulated my imagination long before Mowgli's creation.

Porges also documents the following influences, a list not intended to be complete by any means: Charles Darwin (75), Sir Arthur

Conan Doyle (128), Edward Gibbon (194), Otis Adelbert Kline (474), Booth Tarkington (607), and Mark Twain (606). It need hardly be pointed out, finally, that the pulps of the late nineteenth and early twentieth century must have exercised as much influence on Burroughs as it did on millions of others, none of whom ever wrote a single story.

Themes

Burroughs's themes are likewise to be found in classical as well as contemporary literature.

Appearance versus reality.   One of the most pervasive ones is that of the difference between appearance and reality. Indeed, the whole question of the difference between appearance and reality becomes a major preoccupation for the author in the course of the Tarzan novels, and the protagonist and his jungle world become in turn vehicles for endless variation on it. In the early books, it is most vividly addressed in *Jungle Tales of Tarzan,* where it manifests itself in Tarzan's problematical grappling with the effort to define for himself the distinction between the states of wakefulness and dreaming. The theme is there developed with both humor and an underlying seriousness (129–141).

One very common example of this theme's realization throughout the Tarzan corpus is the distinction repeatedly drawn between the seeming savagery of the jungle and the apparent refinement of civilization, two supposed extremes located at the opposing poles of experience. Nothing, Burroughs repeatedly implies, could be further from the truth. For the savagery of the jungle is all too often seen as a straightforwardness about the realities of the world, while the sophisticated complexities of civilization are taken to task for their deceitfulness and ineradicable hypocrisy. Here the Rousseauistic tradition of the noble savage is not to be dismissed entirely from consideration of the composite characterization of the apeman. The theme is older than Rousseau, however, and was also put to service by many writers who came after the French *philosophe*.

In the context of the present discussion, only a few selected examples will be treated. A most striking one comes from *Tarzan the Invincible* (written in 1927) and involves the mysterious Zora Drinov. Playing out the patterned role of an excessively common motif in the novels, that of a female's abduction by some villain

(human or animal) with erotic designs on her, Zora has been taken
by the great ape To-yat. Tarzan learns of this and sets out to rescue
her. When she recovers her senses she located Tarzan along the
familiar coordinates whereby she has been accustomed to read the
character of "civilized" men: "There had been nothing in the man's
attitude to suggest that he intended to harm her, and yet so accustomed was she to gauge all men by the standards of civilized
society that she could not conceive that he had other than ulterior
designs" (141). She puzzles over his outward appearance, which
seems to belie all her innate suspicions of him. She cannot pin him
down to a set category that will enable her to deal with him, for
everything about her rescuer appears contradictory. He appears wild
and savage but treats her with gentleness and kindness; he seems
mute and incapable of comprehending speech, yet his "intelligent
eyes" do not "even remotely suggest mental or moral degradation"
(141). In short, he upsets all her expectations of men as they have
been molded by civilization, because the

man presented a paradox that intrigued her imagination, seeming, as he
did, so utterly out of place in this savage African jungle; while at the
same time he harmonized perfectly with his surroundings, in which he
seemed perfectly at home and assured of himself. . . . Had he been
unkempt, filthy, and degraded in appearance, she would have catalogued
him immediately as one of those social outcasts, usually half demented,
who are occasionally found far from the haunts of men, living the life of
wild beasts, whose high standards of decency and cleanliness they uniformly
fail to observe. (141)

Supporting the woman's sense of dislocation arising from the dis-
crepancy between her expectations of civilized and uncivilized behavior is the ancillary motif of the raw-and-the-cooked so commonly[11]
incorporated into the larger complex of this theme by Burroughs.
For when Tarzan helps Zora regain her strength, he carefully roasts
the meat he feeds to her, at the same time eating his own raw—
thus once more throwing her off balance about the reality of her
rescuer:

Gradually the girl had been lulled to a feeling of security by the seeming
solicitude of her strange protector. But now distinct misgivings assailed
her, and suddenly she felt a strange new fear of the silent giant in whose

power she was; for when he ate she saw that he ate his meat raw, tearing the flesh like a wild beast. (142)

In this particular novel Burroughs has chosen to underline his great hatred for Russians and especially the Communist variety, for it is these latter, represented by the megalomaniac Zveri, who come to stand for civilization and civilized behavior in contrast to that of the "savage" inhabitants of the jungle. The antithesis is a bit forced, but it does serve to drive home Burroughs's notions about the corruptness and decay of modern man and his civilization. The matter is summed up on the last page of this novel *(Tarzan the Invincible):*

Behind him [viz. Tarzan] followed the four who owed to his humanity more than they could ever know, nor had they known could have [*sic*] guessed that his great tolerance, courage, resourcefulness and the protective instinct that had often safeguarded them sprang not from his human progenitors, but from his lifelong association with the natural beasts of the forest and the jungle, who have these instinctive qualities far more strongly developed than do the unnatural beasts of civilization, in whom the greed and lust of competition have dimmed the luster of these noble qualities where they have not eradicated them entirely. (192)

Religion. Another theme that came to preoccupy Burroughs in the Tarzan novels is that of religion, or, rather, false religion. As has been observed in the previous chapter on the Martian series, religion was an important concern there too, and in particular the unmasking of its more outrageously hypocritical elements. It is important at the outset of this discussion to note that Burroughs was not antireligious, or even anti-Christian. He was, however, opposed to the thick layers of exploitation and abused trust that he saw as encrusting the corpus of legitimate faith. And in this matter no distinction is drawn between Western and African varieties of religion: they are all corrupt and cynical in so far as they are organized and in the manipulative hands of a hieratic caste.

Tarzan himself is surely a religious being, if by religious faith is meant an acknowledgment of the existence of a nontemporal power outside oneself that is sensed to have influence in daily experience. If the term is narrowly conceived to indicate only an obeisance to worldly pomp and circumstance with all its attendant ritual, then Tarzan is equally surely not a religious individual. Early in Tarzan's

life (and early in the series), the apeman comes of necessity to
confront the question of the existence of noncorporeal realities underpinning all the flow and flux manifested in a material world
bound by time. In the sixth book of the series, *Jungle Tales of Tarzan*,
Tarzan finds himself having to deal with questions of religion and
God.[12] It is quite clear that while Tarzan's personal accommodation
with God may not appeal to all, it is undeniably a token of untrammeled religiosity.

It is in this connection of his dawning recognition that something
like a deity exists that the apeman also comes face to face with the
perversion of these inclinations within men. For the sinister witch
doctor Bukawai immediately tarnishes the concept of organized religion and by his behavior exposes its very human greed and lust.
In this Bukawai is but the first in a long line of religious quacks
whom Tarzan will encounter during his spectacular career.

Most venom is reserved for those servants of organized religion
who are also politically influential, for the base of temporary authority enables them to translate private ambitions for power and
wealth into an unabashed exploitation of local credulity. An example
is the powerful ruler and witch doctor Kavandavanda of the Kavuru
in *Tarzan's Quest*. The apeman's wife, Jane, has been captured by a
Kavuru named Ogdli, and when told that she will be taken to
Kavandavanda, she is eager to know who he is: " 'Who is Kavandavanda?' she demanded. 'He is Kavandavanda.' The man spoke as
though that were sufficient explanation. It was as though one said,
'God is God' " (141). When Jane is first led into his throne room,
she is herself almost overcome by a sense of superstitious awe:

Every indolent, contemptuous line of his pose bespoke the autocrat. . . .
Jane could not rid herself of the thought that she was looking upon a
god. . . . Jane felt that she had never looked upon a more beautiful
countenance. An oval face was surmounted by a wealth of golden hair;
below a high, full forehead shone luminous dark eyes that glowed with
the fires of keen intelligence. A perfect nose and a short upper lip completed
the picture of divine beauty that was marred and warped and ruined by
a weak, cruel mouth. (167)

This exquisite monster's claim to divine status is reinforced not only
by the terror he has instilled in his subjects, but also by the immortality that he has achieved. He explains to Jane how he learned
the secret of eternal youth, and requires the bodies (especially the

"glands and blood" [171]) of young women in order to mix his elixir. His own views of God and religion are strictly cynical and self-serving, for he sees the belief in God by others as merely something of value for shaping circumstances to his own private advantage. He holds forth at length to Jane about his own lack of belief in deity, which has in fact been replaced by the idea that he is himself becoming divine (a curiously illogical sequence of thoughts!):

There is no such thing [viz. God]—not yet, at least. . . . Men have imagined a god instead of seeking a god among themselves. They have been led astray by false prophets and charlatans. They have no leader. God should be a leader, and a leader should be a tangible entity—something men can see and feel and touch. He must be mortal and yet immortal. He may not die. He must be omniscient. . . . Almost such as I, Kavandavanda, high priest of the priests of Kavuru. Already am I deathless; already am I omniscient. . . . (171)

Yet this grand schemer is as subject as any of the other priestly pretenders in these novels to his own lusts, in this case for Jane. He wants her to become his goddess, and his concentration on the imagined pleasures of the flesh to the exclusion of attending his religious obligations brings chaos to the Kavuru. At a critical juncture this beautiful impostor is exposed for the fake that he is (187), and in the ensuing melee his immortality is found severely wanting. *Sic semper pontificibus.*

Perhaps the most chilling example of Burroughs's dislike of organized religion comes from the fifteenth novel, *Tarzan Triumphant.* Here we get all the intolerance and cruelty born of religious fanaticism, and by emphasizing what may perhaps be occasional tendencies in men's practice of even the noblest religion, Burroughs has presented an extreme view of piety gone mad. The book begins unlike any of the other novels. In a prologue the reader is taken back to the first century A.D. and the very earliest days of the infant movement that became Christianity. An early convert to the new faith was one Angustus[13] the Ephesian, who is described in less than flattering terms:

Angustus was a young man of moods and epilepsy, a nephew of the house of Onesiphorus. . . . Inclined to fanaticism, from early childhood an epileptic, and worshipping the apostle [viz. Paul of Tarsus] as the representative of the Master of earth, it is not strange that news of the martyrdom of Paul should have so affected Angustus as to seriously imperil his mental balance. (7)

The youth flees to Alexandria, acquiring a "fair haired slave girl from some far northern barbarian tribe" (8) on the island of Rhodes. The prologue ends with "the flight of Angustus and the fair haired slave girl down into Africa from the storied port of Alexandria, through Memphis and Thebae into the great unknown." Burroughs's fascination with Darwinism and the operation of a kind of genetic inevitability in lines of generational descent is well known. The reader may, then, draw inferences from these hints about an epileptic fanatic and his mate, who disappear into the isolation of Africa, about their offspring nearly two thousand years later (cf. page 96: "the curse that had descended to them from Angustus the Ephesian. . . .").

It is into the enclave of the land of South Midian, inhabited by those descendants and ruled by the insane Abraham son of Abraham, that Lady Barbara Collis floats on her parachute. Her mysterious manner of arrival is variously interpreted in this society of super-stitious and enfeebled epileptics. She exploits their superstition so as to elevate herself in their minds to divine status, for she did, after all, descend from heaven without harm (this trick is used also in *Tarzan's Quest* [186–88] in order to impress a superstitious mul-titude). Through a series of plot twists that entail Abraham's crazy if cunning efforts to maintain control over his flock, Lady Collis ends up as sacrificial victim of Jehovah. Wrapped in a net weighted down with rocks, she is hurled into a lake, but escapes through her own considerable courage and initiative. She returns to the village and attempts to reassert her authority as divine, for this time did she not ascend from the depths of the lake unharmed? Unfortunately, her escape from the depths of the lake is seen as the work of the devil, and where water could not destroy her, fire apparently will (90). Rescued this time by one Lafayette Smith, she and her South Midian companion Jezebel escape, only to be captured by men of North Midian.

As if to underscore the difference between genuine religiosity and the adventitious structure of organized religion, Burroughs puts into the mouth of Lady Collis the following thoughts (which should indicate that Burroughs was not antireligious or even anti-Christian as such):

And their religion! Again she shuddered. What a hideous travesty of the teachings of Christ! It was a confused jumble of ancient Christianity and still more ancient Judaism, handed down by word of mouth through a half imbecile people who had no written language; a people who had confused Paul the Apostle with Christ the Master and lost entirely the essence of the Master's teachings, while interpolating hideous barbarisms of their own invention. Sometimes she thought she saw in this exaggerated deviation a suggestion of parallel to other so-called Christian sects of the civilized outer world. (69)

The valley of Midian is itself split into two feuding sects of religious fanatics.[14] The basis for the enmity between these groups of true believers is a point of contention about dogma: did Paul the Apostle have black hair or yellow hair? Captured by the North Midians, Lady Collis and Lafayette Smith are enlightened by the leader Elija on this crucial doctrinal matter:

They [viz. the South Midians] insist that Paul's hair was black, while we know that it was yellow. They are very wicked, blasphemous people. Once long before the memory of man, we were all one people; but there were many wicked heretics among us who had black hair and wished to kill all those with yellow hair; so those with yellow hair ran away and came to the north end of the valley. Ever since, the North Midians have killed all those with black hair and the South Midians all those with yellow hair. Do you think Paul had yellow hair? (149)

In a similar fashion, in the eighth novel *(Tarzan the Terrible)* a strong contrast is set up between the two societies of Pal-ul-don, Ho-don and Waz-don, represented respectively by the white, hairless Ta-den and the hairy, black Om-at. These men and their societies are at eternal war with each other over the question of who is innately superior. Burroughs is clearly and explicitly commenting on the folly of America's racial realities (the book was published in 1921). Thus, listening to the squabbling of his two new-found companions in primitive Pal-ul-don, Ta-den and Om-at,

Tarzan smiled. Even here was the racial distinction between white man and black man—Ho-don and Waz-don. Not even the fact that they appeared to be equals in the matter of intelligence made any difference—one was white and one was black, and it was easy to see that the white considered himself superior to the other—one could see it in his quiet smile. (22)

In the course of this novel Tarzan is able to effect a reconciliation between the antagonists, whose problems are partly religious as well as racial in nature (215).

The religious difficulties encountered by the opposing groups in *Tarzan Triumphant,* then, are emblematic of other social problems which, if gone unheeded, tend to destroy the groups in which they surface. Such issues (e.g., religious animosity, political violence, racial prejudice) are presented in some of the novels and an auctorial position about the folly of such divisiveness, whatever its ultimate source, is advanced. One should surely not underestimate Burroughs's fondness for social criticism in the Tarzan novels, as in the others, be it a central thread unifying a particular book (as in *Tarzan Triumphant*) or merely one of a number of strands woven into the larger fabric of the plot (as in *Tarzan and the Antmen).*

Love.   Since the Tarzan novels are, generically speaking, heroic romances, it is not surprising that love and its darker counterpart, lust, appear again and again in eternal triangles in which, usually, two men vie for the affections of a woman. The woman is subjected to incredible hardships, mistreated by both men and animals (especially apes), but inevitably rises to every occasion and transforms herself into a heroine. Lust and the potential for rape are never far from the surface of the tale, but her escape or rescue from such ardent villainy is predictably regular. Characteristic of the plot configuration in which this theme is made to serve is that found in *Tarzan and the Foreign Legion.* Here the Dutch girl Corrie van der Meer becomes, in turn, the lust object of Japanese soldiers, Sumatran outlaws, and orangutans, and is in turn abducted by each only to escape and be captured once more. Her own passion is for the American pilot Jerry Lucas, who is a confirmed misogynist. He does gradually come around, however, and falls in love with Corrie. He mistakenly believes that she is in love with the young guerilla fighter Tak van der Bos, who, it turns out, is merely a good friend to Corrie through his own wife. In the end, needless to say, the two lovers get married, as good an ending for a romance as any, and pioneered by Tarzan himself at the end of *The Return of Tarzan.* Furthermore, the romance of Jerry Lucas and Corrie van der Meer is paralleled by the one that develops between Tony Rosetti, another confirmed misogynist, and Sarina, who along with Jane, La of Opar, and Nemone of Cathne is one of the more intriguing females to grace the pages of the Tarzan novels. Both Jerry and Tony are changed in the course of their adventures in Sumatra, and the double wedding at the end of the novel underscores the incorporation of these two emotional cripples into normal society. Burroughs appears to have been quite fond of the idea that love changes individuals for the better, and indeed at times has a redemptive quality to it. Thus, in *Tarzan and the Lion Man,* for example, the alcoholic Tom Orman undergoes dramatic change, learning to take on enormous responsibility and, as a result, ending up married to Rhonda Terry. And in *Tarzan Triumphant* the criminal Danny Patrick is transformed by his love for Jezebel of South Midian; this romance is paralleled by the one that develops between Lafayette Smith and Lady Barbara Collis. The parallel love story is in fact a staple of the Tarzan novels, first limned in the second novel *(The Return of Tarzan),* where the blossoming love of Jane Porter and Tarzan is complemented by the parallel developments for Lord Tennington and Jane's friend Hazel Strong. Other examples are found in *Tarzan the Terrible,* where Tarzan's search for his mate is paralleled by Ta-den's for Pan-at-lee, and in *Tarzan and the Lost Empire,* where Erich von Harben's love for Favonia is set side by side with that of Maximus Praeclarus for Dilecta ("the beloved").

Darwinism. A dominant idea in Burroughs's novels and especially the Tarzan series is that of Darwinism. He shared this enthusiasm with many popular and academic writers of his own period, for it is clear[15] that Darwinism made an enormous impact on the literary output of the latter half of the nineteenth and early part of the twentieth century. Tarzan is himself an idealized embodiment of evolutionary development compressed and worked out in a single lifetime. In the very first novel *(Tarzan of the Apes)* the hero is seen as emblem of the emergence of man from primitive ancestors; the society of the apes provides a useful and comprehensible view of popular notions of man's descent from simian forebears. Thus, in that first novel, the legitimacy within the fictional world of what in fact is anthropologically accurate in broad outline is established through commentary on the Dum-Dum, the primitive rites in which the great apes engage from time to time:

From this primitive function has arisen, unquestionably, all the forms and ceremonials of modern church and state, for through all the countless ages, back beyond the uttermost ramparts of a dawning humanity our fierce, hairy forebears danced out the rites of the Dum-Dum to the sound of their earthen drums, beneath the bright light of a tropical moon in the depth of a mighty jungle which stands unchanged today as it stood on that long forgotten night in the dim, unthinkable vistas of the long dead past when our first shaggy ancestors swung from a swaying bough and dropped lightly upon the soft turf of the first meeting place. (52)

Prior to this generalization about the group, Burroughs had insisted rather unequivocally on the Darwinian reading that is to be given to Tarzan himself. For in describing the apechild's laborious efforts to learn to read, the author had also placed heavy emphasis on this emblematic element in Tarzan's literary persona: "Tarzan of the Apes, little primitive man, presented a picture filled, at once, with pathos and with promise—an allegorical figure of the primordial groping through the black night of ignorance toward the light of learning" (48).

In connection with this Darwinian leitmotiv coursing through the novels it is necessary to say something about Burroughs's general treatment of women and blacks (and other ethnic groups). From the vantage of the mid-1980s many of the comments about blacks and situations in which they are placed are, if not overtly racist, certainly very patronizing. As we have noted above, however, Burroughs was keenly aware of the racist nature of American society. At the same time, many of the unexamined presuppositions that underpin the picture of blacks that emerges from the novels are no longer acceptable to public taste and do not, properly, appear in popular or even academic forms of entertainment. But just as Aristotle's approval of slavery is not necessarily a reason to throw out Aristotle, Burroughs's acceptance of contemporary social and cultural prejudices that are no longer publicly permissible is insufficient justification for condemning his works. In portraying blacks by and large as he did,[16] he merely reflects societal norms and indeed the pronouncements of contemporary scholars and molders of public opinion.[17] His overwhelmingly patronizing views of blacks and other groups (including women) is no more acceptable than, for example, are the portrayals of blacks in radio and film before, say, the late sixties, or in early television (e.g., "Amos and Andy").

But it is undeniable that to the extent that he "Darwinized" the Tarzan novels, Burroughs implies more than once that white American and Western European (most notably British) stock is the pinnacle of evolutionary trends, and other national and racial groups are somehow lacking by comparison. Yet, in a novel like *Tarzan the Terrible,* as we noted above, there is unmistakable criticism of contemporary attitudes toward blacks. Again, it is surely to the point here to recall that on Mars, the first race was not the white race, but the black, and from it are descended all others.[18]

Eugenics. Burroughs's fascination with eugenics is undoubtedly tied to his strong interest in Darwinism. Tarzan himself is often said to be the end-development of generations of British aristocratic stock, representing what Burroughs seems to have conceived of as the ne plus ultra of eugenic perfection. This point is in fact made concerning Tarzan's father, Lord Greystoke, on the second page of the first novel *(Tarzan of the Apes):* "Clayton was the type of Englishman that one likes best to associate with the noblest monuments of historic achievement upon a thousand victorious battlefields—a strong, virile man—mentally, morally, physically." And throughout the entire corpus of Tarzan novels the father of Tarzan hovers constantly in the immediate background as a kind of symbol of Tarzan's descent from a long line of aristocratic ancestors. The ever-present physical emblem of this heritage is the great knife that had belonged to his father and which, together with Tarzan's human intelligence, first enabled him to gain physical superiority over beasts many times stronger than himself. Nor is the line of descent at an end with Tarzan, for it continues fully recognizable in the character of Tarzan's son Jack, also known as Korak the Killer, who is featured in the fourth novel, *The Son of Tarzan.* In this transparent bildungsroman the youngest Greystoke recapitulates in broad strokes the growth and development of his father, Tarzan, undertaking his own kind of odyssey to attain maturity.

Eugenics as public policy is a striking feature of the novel entitled *Tarzan and the Antmen.* Echoing both Aristophanes and Swift in its satiric analysis of social organization, this book[19] relies on elements of science fiction to make its plot go. In this respect it conjures up most precisely of all the Tarzan novels the kind of fantastic assumptions that so frequently buttress the stories about Mars and Venus. For Tarzan is reduced to the antmen's eighteen-inch height by the "greatest mind in Veltopismakus," Zoanthrohago, the "scientist who works miracles" (104). This genius has invented the instrumentation by means of which living matter is proportionally reduced, and Tarzan, captured in a battle between the forces of Veltopismakus and Trohanadalmakus, is the first human used for his experimentation. Having become like them in stature, Tarzan is able to observe from the inside the workings of these two societies of Minunians. Veltopismakus is a community given over to luxurious living and an emphasis on external display, while the Trohanadalmakusians are hard-working and highly efficient, concerned with underlying substance rather than empty show. The point is made most eloquently by Komodoflorensal, son of the king of Trohanadalmakus, who characterizes the distinction between the two groups as follows:

I have heard that Elkomoelhago's [viz. the king of Veltopismakus] troops are famous for the perfection of their drill, and as justly so as is Veltopismakus for the beauty of her walks and gardens; but, my friend, these very things constitute the weakness of the city. While Elkomoelhago's warriors are practicing to perfect their appearance upon parade, the warriors of my father, Adendrohahkis, are far afield, out of sight of admiring women and spying slaves, practicing the art of war under the rough conditions of the field and the camp. . . . it was not long since you saw less than fifteen thousand Trohanadalmakusians repulse fully thirty thousand warriors of Veltopismakus. . . . Yes, they can drill beautifully upon parade . . . but they have not been trained in the sterner arts of war—it is not the way of Elkomoelhago. He is soft and effeminate. (112)[20]

The essential difference between the two Minunian realms has its basis in genetics. At an earlier point in the novel Komodoflorensal, who is a kind of local cicerone for Tarzan the stranger, had explained something of the social customs and history of Trohanadalmakus. "Ages ago" in a memorable battle the population had been almost eradicated because of the warriors' lack of stamina; only the help of their slaves (who were mostly of nonlocal descent) with their much greater endurance had saved the city. The following explanation was offered by a survivor:

of all the race of Minunians the people of the city of Trohanadalmakus were the most ancient and . . . for ages there had been no infusion of new blood, since they were not permitted to mate outside their own caste, while the slaves, recruited from all the cities of Minuni, had interbred, with the result that they had become strong and robust while their masters, through inbreeding, had grown correspondingly weaker. . . . For us of the royal family it has been nothing less than salvation from extinction. Our ancestors were transmitting disease and insanity to their progeny. The new, pure, virile blood of the slaves has washed the taint from our veins and so altered has our point of view become that whereas, in the past, the child of a slave woman and a warrior was without caste, the lowest of the low, now they rank highest of the high, since it is considered immoral for one of the royal family to wed other than a slave. (55–56)

The current situation in the city promotes a kind of weeding out of the weakest of the recent prisoners and their children, who are forced to undertake "labor from which the limit of human endurance was exacted . . . fully fifty percent of them were literally worked to death. With the second generation the education of the children commenced. . . ." Although the planned eugenics of the antmen society is the most thoroughly conceived example of social planning in the Tarzan novels, the theme appears elsewhere also, testifying to Burroughs's curiosity about spinning out various mechanical scenarios based on it.

In the two cities of Nimmr and the Sepulcher (in the lost valley of the Sepulcher in *Tarzan, Lord of the Jungle*), for example, a rational mechanism has been worked out for mutual exchanges in order to prevent too closed a pattern of breeding. They formally suspend hostilities to celebrate the Great Tourney, which presented an opportunity for the selection of exogamous brides:

The genesis of the custom, which was now fully seven centuries old, doubtless lay in the wise desire of some ancient Gobred or Bohun to maintain the stock of both factions strong and virile by the regular infusion of new blood, as well, perhaps, as to prevent the inhabitants of the two cities from drifting too far apart in manners, customs and speech. (126)

Another such lost enclave with two antithetical and hostile communities (Castra Sanguinarius and Castrum Mare) is found in *Tarzan and the Lost Empire*. Erich von Harben is remarking on the notable lack of criminals in the city of Castrum Mare, and gets an explanation from his guide, Mallius. When the city was first founded almost two millenia ago, it was overrun with criminals and cut-throats, and the first emperor instituted a drastic policy of genetic laundering that manifested itself as a type of euthanasia for the greater good of the polity:

he made laws so drastic that no thief or murderer lived to propagate his kind. Indeed, the laws of Honus Hasta destroyed not only the criminal, but all the members of his family, so that there was none to transmit to posterity the criminal inclinations of a depraved sire. . . . the laws of Honus Hasta prevented the breeding of criminals. (53)

In *Tarzan and the Lion Man*, the "god of England" was born in 1833 and graduated from Oxford in 1855; he came under the influence of the evolutionary theories of Lamarck and Darwin, and had studied in Austria with the geneticist Mendel. In Africa he used his knowledge to assure his own immortality by using ape-cells and remaking apes into humans by giving them human cells. He thus created a community of humanoid apes and has himself become increasingly simian—immortal to be sure, but at the same time like the apes in appearance. The cells of Tarzan and the beautiful Rhonda will, he hopes, stay this seemingly inevitable bestialization: "I sought some means to prolong my own [viz. life] and to bring back youth. At last I was successful. I discovered how to segregate body cells and transfer them from one individual to another. I used young gorillas of both sexes and transplanted their virile, youthful body cells to my own body" (136).

If, finally, one accepts that one of the many roles or functions of science fiction is to extrapolate from contemporary realities alternative possibilities for social organization and human inventiveness, Burroughs's thematic preoccupations move at least a portion of the Tarzan novels into the mainstream of science fiction. We have singled out some of the more prominent themes that course throughout the Tarzan novels. At the same time it is impossible to do justice to all of them, and it must suffice merely to alert the reader to those that are most conspicuous.

But it is time to turn to a closer look at Tarzan himself and attempt to outline just what it was Burroughs fashioned when he created this, his most enduring character.

Chapter Four
Tarzan: Characters

The Tarzan who emerges from the novels that Burroughs wrote rather than the movies that Hollywood dreamed up is a fairly complicated personality. As we have seen in the previous chapter, there can be little question that whatever his more immediate ancestors in the literary climate of Burroughs's own day and age may have been, he was certainly cast very much in the mold of the mythological heroes of antiquity. Some of the more striking points of contact must be indicated at this stage.

Hero

Master of animals. No doubt the most notable feature of Tarzan is his unusual yet familiar association with the world of animals, in particular that of the great apes. Brought up by them, he of course speaks their language and knows the customs and habits of their tribal life. Affinity with animals is a common characteristic of heroes, and indeed in some mythologies (notably Amerindian ones) the lines of demarcation between animal and heroic man are often blurred at best. The motif is pervasive enough among classical heroes, as for example in the case of Achilles and his talking horses, Bellerophon and his winged steed, Odysseus and his dog, and Dionysus and his leopards.

In his own mind, even in the years of adulthood, Tarzan thinks of the great she-ape Kala as his real mother, and not the Hon. Alice Rutherford who was his biological mother. As if to balance the equation, so to speak, in his own mind Tarzan's father is never Tublat, the mate of Kala, but Lord John Greystoke, who was his biological father. The latter's presence is ubiquitous in the novels in the ever-present emblem of the great knife that Tarzan as child discovered in the cabin his father had built by the sea before the apeman was born. This stated dual parentage has interesting implications for our reading of Tarzan as hero.

It is demonstrable that the heroes of classical mythology have a dual provenience—indeed, that is part of what it means, in a technical sense, to be a classical hero. They have one foot in the divine world and one in the human world, for each hero has one divine and one human parent. Nor does it matter whether it is the father who is divine (as is Heracles's father Zeus, whose mortal partner Alcmene bore the hero) or the mother (as is Aeneas's mother Aphrodite, who was made pregnant by the mortal hunter Anchises). What Burroughs has done here is to adapt the ancient pattern to the exigencies of his own fictive world, and so gave his heroic protagonist a human and nonhuman *set* of parents. That Tarzan should have been born of an ape and a human is of course the kind of baroque monstrousness that is by and large foreign to the Tarzan novels,[1] if not entirely to the Martian stories. And further, rather than making his hero share in the divine world, Burroughs makes him participate in the world of animals. Thus, the general notion of a hero coming from two distinct worlds is adapted to the Darwinian overtones of the novels. In this sense Tarzan is both unequivocally traditional and at the same time something of an innovation on an ancient theme. It is likewise clear in these novels that Burroughs attributes to the animals the kind of respect and idealized comportment that was associated with the mythological deities of antiquity. Yet, in a similar vein, he reserves the right to portray some of them as undesirable. It may be surmised that some part of Tarzan's enormous appeal to men and women of all ages and levels of education is a function of this role of "missing link" that he fulfills.

Physical traits.   The physical Tarzan is not much different from many heroic types of antiquity, down to the partial disfigurement. For like Odysseus, who had a great scar running along his thigh from a youthful battle with a great boar, Tarzan has the famous scar running along the hairline of his forehead, sustained in a youthful battle against a gorilla. The apeman's stamina and bodily prowess are addressed with regularity on virtually every page that he appears, and such external criteria of heroism he has in common with a Heracles or an Achilles. His skill as warrior and fighter with a number of different weapons is typically that of a number of heroes: thus, Odysseus's special abilities with his great bow is a well-known feature of that hero, as are those of Tarzan the archer.[2]

Additional features in the composite makeup of the apeman point likewise to the mythic origins from which Tarzan is created. The highly unusual circumstances of his birth on the wild shore of Africa, his status as foundling when his foster mother, the great ape Kala, first comes upon him, his nurture and rearing by animals, the early recognition of his specialness among his own "people" as well as, later, among human beings, his formulaic involvements with tempting females, his encounters with monsters both animal and human, his bridging of different worlds—these are some of the unmistakably mythic and folkloristic echoes.

Mental dimension. But of even greater significance in the literary Tarzan is the character's intellectual or mental traits. A general perception of Tarzan, created by the movies, is that he is a semiliterate barely capable of monosyllabic grunts to make his simple wants known. The Tarzan Burroughs actually created is eloquent, highly intelligent, and well-read. A superb linguist, Tarzan was never at a loss for word or thought on any subject. His comfortable taciturnity where talk would have been merely mindless prattle, however, may well be the false foundation on which Hollywood built up a personality devoid of a third dimension. But no one can read the novels without gaining some sense of a lively intelligence, humor, and thoughtfulness at work in the apeman.

Surely a most striking instance of this aspect of Tarzan's persona is the prodigious feat of learning that he undertook as a child. Unaided by pedagogues or schools he plunged into the world of books he had discovered in his father's cabin and proceeded, slowly and with great labor to be sure, to teach himself to read. Books opened up a whole new world of realities to his inquisitive mind, and this novel kind of excitement is a thrill that never quite leaves him. Thus, when he first reaches civilization under the careful scrutiny of the French lieutenant Paul D'Arnot, the marvels of museums and libraries in Paris transfix the apeman. In *The Return of Tarzan* Burroughs describes Tarzan's delight and despair in terms that well capture the youthful intellectual's ambivalence toward his recognition of the finiteness of man and the boundlessness of knowledge, learning, and art:

Tarzan spent the two following weeks renewing his former brief acquaintance with Paris. In the daytime he haunted the libraries and picture galleries. He had become an omnivorous reader, and the world of possibilities that were opened to him in this seat of culture and learning fairly appalled him when he contemplated the very infinitesimal crumb of the sum total of human knowledge that a single individual might hope to acquire even after a lifetime of study and research. (25–26)

Tarzan is also a trickster. The trickster as type is of venerable vintage in myth and folklore, and of the many classical heroes in whom this aspect is most visible, Odysseus is a prime example. The general shape of the trickster's personality is drawn in strokes that highlight the qualities of mental adventurism and overreaching cunning, as well as boundless appetite for material and sexual satisfaction; in many mythological systems, most notably African and Amerindian, the trickster frequently has an animal incarnation, showing up as coyote, spider, muskrat, and other types of "clever" creatures. Another side of the trickster's great mental energy is his role as culture hero, a folkloristic type whose primary function is to help bring a given society its laws, institutions, and learning. In this capacity the trickster reveals the nurturing and beneficial side of his essentially double personality.

In the case of Tarzan the trickster, it is this mental component that is accentuated by Burroughs, although the hero's potential for erotic entanglements are ever present if rarely realized. As trickster he is as much culture hero as he is prankster, in particular with reference to his own tribe of apes. For after he kills the king, Kerchak, and becomes leader of the group he proceeds to introduce a number of favorable practices into their communal life. He cannot, however, quite rise above the powerful impulse to play a kind of monitory joke on his fellows. The most immediate manifestation of tricksterism in the apeman is this mercurial sense of humor with its strong overtones of practical joking. And like all practical jokers (and tricksters especially), Tarzan too finds that fun directed against others can boomerang. Things backfire, sometimes dangerously, in ways not considered by the initiator, and Tarzan learns this in most humiliating and potentially death-threatening fashion in an illustrative passage from *Jungle Tales of Tarzan*.

Because the apes lacked any form of warning system, a member of the tribe is killed by a lion. Tarzan tries to remedy this unnecessary exposure of the apes to risk by establishing sentries to hold watch while the rest of the group forages locally for food. In the dual role of joke-playing prankster and testing culture-hero Tarzan here gets himself into a great deal of trouble, which almost proves his undoing. Donning the skin of a lion he creeps up on the unwary tribe in order to test the sentries and have a little joke, hoping to frighten them when the see the "lion." Unfortunately he has miscalculated the sense of dedication shown by the guards. For they not only sound a general alert but proceed to kill the intruding "lion," and had not a little monkey intervened to reveal to the frenzied apes that the object of their rage is Tarzan in disguise, the apeman probably would have been killed. His reaction, upon reflection, to the experience is surely typical of the trickster type:

It made Tarzan very glad to know these things; but at the other lesson he had been taught he reddened. He had always been a joker, the only joker in the grim and terrible company; but now as he lay there half dead from his hurts, he almost swore a solemn oath forever to forego practical joking—almost, but not quite. (128)

Mental processes of a more strictly intellectual type are likewise far from lacking in the apeman. The incidents described in the course of *Jungle Tales of Tarzan* speak forcefully to the point, for here Tarzan grapples with the issues of good and evil, and the distinctions between what is illusory and what is objectively real. And among the many interests that Tarzan does have, none is perhaps more intense or more consistently sustained than his passion for languages. It is clear that Burroughs, himself, had an interest in the grammatical particulars of ape-language, for in *Jungle Tales of Tarzan,* again, he provides a rather comprehensive conspectus of the basic organizing principles of the language (it displays notable similarities in both syntax and morphology to classical Greek and Latin!).

Much remains that could be said about Burroughs's Tarzan, but the broad outlines of the literary persona should emerge distinctly from the observations made above. Above all it is necessary for the uninitiated reader to make a conscious effort to put aside those prejudices about Tarzan picked up from movies, television, and, though to a much smaller degree, the comics.[3]

Villains

Every hero needs his villain, for only through the comparison, whether explicitly invited or implicitly suggested, between hero and villain does the heroism of the former emerge in its full intensity. The same may, and should, also be stated in regard to the villain:

his villainy is limned all the more sharply in juxtaposition to his opponent's nobleness. The villain is thus always an important character, in a sense as central to the narrative as the hero, for the one is not much without the other. And indeed there are times when the villain displays what may best be termed a kind of inverted heroism, a grandness on his own terms.

Such a conception of villain and villainy does not require the villain to be human (as is often the case in the Tarzan stories), or even animate. A part of the hero may play the role of villain (commonly realized by the use of twins, one good and one bad) to the hero himself, or some relative may be the opponent, or the villain may even be an emblematic force of nature (destructive storm, deadly jungle, impenetrable mountain pass) against which the hero must pit himself and emerge victorious, usually after suffering a temporary setback. Nor is it uncommon to find that there often are suggestive similarities between a hero and his animate opponents, not the least important of which may be kinship.

In the Tarzan stories there is certainly no dearth of villains. They come in many shapes, nationalities, and forms of life. At times they are African blacks, at other times European whites; sometimes they are human, sometimes animal; now they are the impersonal threats of a withering desert or an engulfing sea, now they are the personified malevolence of the jungle. In the particular case of Tarzan, moreover, it is not an exaggeration to nominate so-called civilized society and her hypocritical members as chief villain in the gallery of rogues parading in and out of the stories.

Whatever or whoever the antagonist of the moment may be, he is not drawn with subtlety. Contrasts between personalities as well as issues are boldly and unambiguously defined, and the reader of the Tarzan books need rarely be troubled by a sense of moral uncertainty about a given character. Ability to tolerate ambiguity of the sort encountered in contemporary popular literature (e.g., John Le Carre, Ross MacDonald, Eric Ambler) is not necessary here. But it must at the same time be noted that a seeming villain in a Tarzan story not infrequently turns out to be quite the opposite, or in the course of the story undergoes some kind of recognition or awakening that impels him to a moral reordering of values. This redemptive quality to the characterization of many a Burroughs villain is a function of an essentially optimistic view of the changeability of human nature in individuals, and itself stands in refreshing contrast to Burroughs's generally unrelieved pessimism about the folly and turpitude of man in the collective.

Typology. Of great interest are the many named and characterized villains with whom Tarzan comes in contact once he has reached adulthood. These are human more often than not, although there are numerous animals represented among them.

A typology of these "bad guys" is readily ascertainable, and it collapses significant distinctions between men and animals: either sort is bestial. The Russian expatriate Rokoff is an early example of the "civilized" monsters (in *The Return of Tarzan*), as is Canler (in *Tarzan of the Apes*), Tarzan's rival in his wooing of Jane Porter. Both exhibit features typical of the Burroughs villain: arrogance and delusions of grandeur, limitless avarice and an uncontrollable sexual lust, and a cruelty and ruthlessness utterly insensitive to individuals who "get in the way." Although the corrosive ambitions of a Canler or a Rokoff are not conspicuously political in orientation, in many of the villains of later books the delusion of grandeur has been cranked up to a blazing megalomania holding or yearning to hold entire societies in thrall. Typical examples are the mad scientist in *Tarzan and the Lion Man* or the crazed fanatic Abraham[4] in *Tarzan Triumphant*.

Billings and civilization. The first villain proper that we meet in the Tarzan novels is the infamous Captain Billings of the ship transporting Lord and Lady Greystoke, Tarzan's future parents, to West Africa. Though he appears only briefly and only at the beginning of the first novel *(Tarzan of the Apes)*, he is in many ways a typical Burroughs villain: awesome in appearance, physically cruel, a bully compensating for inborn cowardice, loathed and feared by his fellows and underlings, and a deserving candidate for the unpleasant death he suffers at the hands of those he has tormented. This pattern is the basis for a number of variations on villainy, and subsequent exemplars remain remarkably true to this basic coding.

Important here is the recognition that the captain is in truth *not* the first villain, for that distinction is reserved for a "friendly European power." Her emissaries in Africa were abusing the natives to whom they were supposedly bringing European law and manners. To attempt to remedy this malfeasance Lord Greystoke is sent out from England, and so the course of Tarzan's life is set in motion by the very villainy of civilization that he condemned from his very first encounter with it.

Tublat and other animals.   The first real villains with whom
the young Tarzan must contend are his foster-father, Tublat, mate
of Kala, and the great Bolgani, or gorilla.[5] His unexpected success
against Bolgani is a function of his father's knife, and he employs
similar methods against Tublat. In late adolescence he overpowers
Kerchak, king of the tribe, and himself becomes the leader of the
group. In addition to these individual monsters against whom Tarzan does mortal combat is a host of generic foes that prowl the
jungle and threaten Tarzan's security, prime among whom are Sheeta
the leopard, Sabor the lioness, and Numa the lion. These encounters
tend to be highly formulaic,[6] a kind of generalized backdrop of
lurking violence against which the actions of Tarzan as both child
and man are played out.

Xerstle and other functionaries.   We should take a closer look
at one of the more unsavory humans, Xerstle of *Tarzan and the City
of Gold.* He is first met in the book when he is ousted from his
quarters to make room for the stranger, Tarzan. Elevated through
political preferments rather than innate ability, Xerstle is a ruthless
hustler on the make, and his erstwhile roommate's characterization
of him is accurate enough: "Xerstle is a rat—like his friend, Erot"
(89). When the machinations of this nasty pair seem to go awry,
it is Xerstle who dreams up the scheme of the grand lion hunt as
a cover for getting rid of Tarzan. There is an element of cunning
in Xerstle's plan, but he is in the end outwitted by the apeman,
and finds the tables turned on him. Indeed, it is trickster Tarzan
who plays a game with the unwitting villain and places him in an
embarrassing position. The network of villains and villainy of which
Xerstle is a part is unraveled by the apeman, and their plans remain
unfulfilled.

Like Xerstle, the human villains in the novels tend to operate in
groups, hankering for political power, sexual favors, wealth, or a
combination of these. As part of a clique engaged in illegally main-
taining or promoting such advantages at the expense of a larger
collective, these villains invariably give off a strong antidemocratic,
profascist odor. Operating collectively, they stand in sharp relief to
Tarzan, whose most effective action is taken on a personal initiative
unconcerned with anticipatory measures for deflecting blame in the
event of failure. A Xerstle is a minor functionary of a larger political
and hieratic structure, but even absolute rulers (e.g., Sublatus in
Tarzan and the Lost Empire) must depend on the group and thus may

fall because of it. To be sure, Tarzan has his animals, especially the apes and Tantor the elephant, in addition to the loyal Waziri, to help him when the occasion arises, but here the difference is that Tarzan never plays the tyrant or autocrat with them, and hence can count on their support. Villains, or the faction to which they are party, tend to be bested as much by their own weaknesses as by the bottled resentments of subjects and colleagues. It almost seems as though Burroughs were suggesting that such collective villainy is foredoomed to lapse on internal grounds.

It is therefore noteworthy that animal villains are basically lone operators. Believing as he did in a very American code of rugged individualism and also holding a generally pessimistic view of mankind, Burroughs perhaps meant to elevate even villainous animals above their human analogues simply by making them individualistic wrongdoers. For when we do find a group of animal villains, as in the case of the English-speaking apes in *Tarzan and the Lion Man,* we see that on the inside they have become more human than initial observation of their appearance might lead one to expect. These various physical and psychological monsters are as much intended to convey Burroughs's attitudes about "civilization" as to provide narrative excitement. They invite comparison between their own bungling attempts to hold onto unlawful and evil privilege, and Tarzan's effortless individualism and leadership in depriving them of favored status in their respective societies, be they African, as in *Jungle Tales of Tarzan,* Arab, as in *Tarzan Lord of the Jungle,* European, as in *Tarzan and the Golden Lion,* Japanese, as in *Tarzan and the Foreign Legion,* or even fabled, as in *Tarzan and the City of Gold.*

Heroines

Who are the heroines of the Tarzan tales?

Is it Jane, his wife? Or the beautiful La of Opar? The diabolical Nemone of Cathne? Practical women like Corrie van der Meer or Lady Barbara Collis? Romantics like Rhonda Terry? Or perhaps mothers, like the great she-ape Kala or the native Momaya? Or even potential villainesses like Sarina or Zora Drinov who in the end turn out "good"?

Although many women in the novels are portrayed as the "weaker sex," it is equally clear that Burroughs displayed as wide a range in his portrayal of women as he did in the case of other characters,

heroic or villainous, animal or human. And just as there are numerous characters who are merely unpleasant, there is no lack of
women whose main traits are a general offensiveness (like the impossible Penelope Leigh [*Tarzan and the Castaways*] or the unpleasant
Naomi Madison). The given types share features, to be sure, and
generic similarities are recognizable, but each is an individual and
endowed by the author with particularizing detail. As types, then,
they may be said to sort themselves into four large categories: nurturer, lover, independent, and vamp. This taxonomy is merely
suggestive, since it is obvious that some of the more complex characters display aspects of more than one type. Thus, Jane, for example, is as much lover as nurturer, and La as much vamp as lover.
In this section we shall consider in more detail the following individuals: Kala, the ape-mother of Tarzan; Jane, the wife of Tarzan;
and Nemone, the haughty and unbalanced queen of Cathne (in
Tarzan and the City of Gold.)

   Kala.   Kala the ape dies fairly early in the first book of the
series, *Tarzan of the Apes,* yet hovers like an invisible presence
throughout Tarzan's life. She is mentioned at least once in almost
every book, a mark of the importance that she occupied in the
transformation of the helpless baby into strapping youth. One need
not read autobiographical detail on Burroughs's part into the portrait
of this quintessentially maternal character, nor should one feel com-
pelled to view the depiction of Tarzan's intractable relationship with
his foster father, Tublat, mate of Kala, as in any sense indicative
of the author's attitude toward his own father, George Tyler Burroughs. Although some suggestion to this effect has been made,[7]
the biographical tradition of criticism has, happily, waned in recent
years, and little effort should be given over to attempts at analyzing
Burroughs's childhood or family constellation on the basis of what
appears in his novels. Although the relationship between Tarzan
and Tublat is highly charged and results in the latter's death at
Tarzan's hands, the fact remains that from earliest childhood Burroughs remained "secure within a close-knit circle of family and
friends" (*ERB,* 9) and enjoyed all the material and emotional com-
forts of a prosperous upper middle-class family. We do know that
at the early age of eleven Burroughs had become enamored of Greek
mythology (*ERB,* 12), which is quite clearly the source for the grid
in which the triangular relationship of child and parents is here
mapped. It is typically mythological, found in the biographies of

hundreds of classical heroes: a cruel and resentful male (father, uncle, grandfather, or analogous authority figure) tries to destroy the child in spite of protests or protective measures taken by the nurturing mother; at some point after the child has become an adult the mother may have to be protected from the male parent, who either effects a reconciliation with the hero or is killed, often by the hero himself. Whatever the ultimate provenience of this pattern may be in the early history of human kind, it is deeply embedded in our consciousness. It may represent a kind of tribal autobiography, preserved and perpetuated in myth, which would help to explain why the relationship between Kala and Tarzan over against Tublat impresses the reader so powerfully.

Kala herself is surely one of the most sympathetically drawn of all the characters in the Tarzan stories. In an ongoing series of comparisons with Tarzan's biological mother, Lady Alice, the great ape emerges to no disadvantage. Her maternal instincts and anthropomorphized love for her adopted son make her as touching an exemplar of motherhood as any found in the entire corpus.[8] As long as Tarzan is helpless, even hopelessly retarded by the standards applicable to the development of the other infants in the tribe of Kerchak the ape, his mother protects him with a fierce loyalty against the many hazards besetting him. When he is almost killed by Bolgani the gorilla, it is only through the self-denying sacrifice of her own good health that she is able to devote sufficient attention to him to prevent him from dying. At the same time she is not above cuffing him or disciplining him if his education in jungle lore or socialization into the tribe requires it. And when Tarzan does start to develop mentally and brightly outshine his age-mates in the cleverness of games devised and hunting strategies conceived, Kala's heart swells with maternal pride. Burroughs idealizes the concept of mother in Kala, striking just the right balance between motherly nurture, love, and physical comforting on the one hand, and, on the other, strictness, discipline and, at the right time, letting go. One can readily appreciate that Tarzan's supreme sense of self-confidence in later life derives in no small measure from the nourishing presence of Kala during earlier years.

The fact that Kala is an ape and Tarzan a man-child points up a significant feature of the mythic patterning that underpins the characterization of this heroine. For she is like many a heroine of classical myth in that the mother and the son come from distinct stocks: if the mother is a goddess, the son is a mortal, and subject to all the limitations of mortality; help from the powerful mother is, however, a constant in this grouping, as the famous instance of mortal Achilles and immortal Thetis, his mother, demonstrates. Kala is not at all different from these goddess heroines in her concern for and devotion to her "different" son than these divine literary prototypes, and her very name, Kala, which means "beautiful female" in classical Greek, is a common epithet for heroines both mortal and immortal in classical mythology. Her lineage, then, is an ancient one, and her portrayal by Burroughs in the opening few pages of the first novel locate her squarely in the larger heroic tradition of which Tarzan himself is such a remarkable descendant.

Jane Porter.   Although women do appear in the novels who are unmistakably conceived of as the "weaker sex," Jane Clayton, Lady Greystoke, née Porter, is not one of them. She is above all what we may call spunky; a dependence that does not cling and allows for the display of personal initiative characterizes her relationship to Tarzan. A well-developed personality in her own right, she is curiously missing from the large majority of the later works. The reader meets her in the course of the tempestuous romance and eventual marriage in the first two books (*Tarzan of the Apes* and *The Return of Tarzan*). She undergoes the harrowing pressure of her son's kidnapping as an infant in *The Beasts of Tarzan* and his disappearance to Africa in *The Son of Tarzan,* is abducted by slavers in the fifth book (*Tarzan and the Jewels of Opar*), is completely absent in the next one *Jungle Tales of Tarzan,* and appears as victim of German savagery in *Tarzan the Untamed* and *Tarzan the Terrible.* In *Tarzan and the Golden Lion* she undertakes, herolike, a quest in search of the missing Tarzan, and makes a good showing of what she has learned from Tarzan. As she tells her son when she sets out: "You know that my jungle-craft, while not equal to that of Tarzan or Korak, is by no means a poor asset, and that, surrounded by the loyalty and bravery of the Waziri, I shall be safe" (130). Thereafter she is a genuine character in only one other novel, the nineteenth (*Tarzan's Quest*), where she displays the wonted presence of mind, which helps to insure her own safety and that of her companions. Thus, in roughly two thirds of the novels she is not a character and is in fact not even mentioned.

Burroughs created in her a delightful and sympathetic portrait of the perfect mate for the apeman, but she is not central to the extended mythos of the hero. Tarzan, of course, is, and continued featuring of his mate may well have seemed an unwise strategy for the author to pursue. No one character should compete with the apeman for attention, and Jane at times bids fair to do so (as in *The Return of Tarzan* and *The Beasts of Tarzan,* for example). Only in one other novel, *The Son of Tarzan,* does a character other than Tarzan clearly dominate the action, and here it is the son, Jack (a.k.a. Korak the Killer), whose carefully crafted bildungsroman recapitulates the ontogeny of the father, thus in effect acting out a displaced version of Tarzan's own growth and development into adulthood. It may well be that Jane, once conceived and linked to the apeman, developed into a character who proved too successful to be allowed full access to all the novels.

The reader first meets Jane Porter when she is shipwrecked with a party at the same spot where, a generation earlier, Tarzan's parents had been set ashore by the mutinous crew of the *Fuwalda.* She is an American, from Baltimore, and the daughter of Professor Archimedes Q. Porter, a bungling and unworldly academic. A suit is being pressed on her by the Englishman, William Cecil Clayton; he is Tarzan's cousin, and the most civilized of a subsequent parade of wooers who sue for her affections by fair means and foul. Few women have been subjected to a more sustained assault on their virtue than Jane, and few, one dares say, have been more resolute in deflecting and defusing these ardent aspirers. Beginning with the first novel, the author sets forth a kind of programmatic version of the levels of cunning eroticism that will continue to beset her throughout her career. The civilized variety of which William Cecil Clayton is the most sympathetic representative is dwarfed by the monstrous breeds of lust and greed that pursue her for differing ends. The shady extremes are already adumbrated in the first novel in the repellent personalities of the great ape Terkoz, a foster brother to Tarzan, and the oily Baltimore businessman, Canler; these two scoundrels, different as they surely are in appearance and background, are in reality lusting brothers under the skin, and both are dealt a summary kind of justice by Tarzan in his own suit of Jane. The assaults continue in the second book, most notably in the person of the Russian knave Rokoff, and in the third, in that of the cannibal chief M'ganwazam, who would sell her or keep her for himself. The assailants are "civilized" Europeans, African natives, and deranged apes,[9] and they all give Jane abundant opportunity to display her coolness under pressure and, indeed, a growing sense of self-sufficiency and independence of action. In the last book in which she has a major role *(Tarzan's Quest)* she is something of an initiator and guide for action that must be taken in order to assure the survival of the party to which she belongs. This forceful and strong-willed woman, filled with courage and resolution, is quite a different personality from the young, swooning girl we meet in the first novel, and there is a genuine sense of her development and maturation into an independent, even self-sufficient, character who is the fit and worthy spouse of Tarzan. Association with her husband is partially responsible for this transformation, for he has taught her much about jungle lore and the ways of wild animals, knowledge that enables her to persevere and survive where others would die. As wife of the lord of the jungle, himself established by Burroughs as godlike, it is consistent that Jane, too, be compared to a divinity. Thus, in chapter 16 of *Tarzan the Terrible* Burroughs describes in detail the practical resourcefulness of Jane alone in the jungle and facing various animal and human opponents, and, with more than a token nod, entitles the chapter "Diana of the Jungle."

Nemone. Nemone of Cathne in *Tarzan and the City of Gold* is, very briefly, a woman of striking oppositions. Where Kala is essentially a nurturer and Jane a supporter, Nemone is a destroyer, a kind of bitch-queen who will annihilate what she cannot have. And since Tarzan is having none of her, he is to be put to the lions, who are bred for such sport by the nobles of Cathne, the City of Gold.

A combination of the destructive aspects of a Circe-type and the seductive charms of an odalisque, this childlike and unstable regent makes an indelible impression on the reader. Unlike La of Opar, whom she most closely resembles in the other tales, she appears in only this one novel; the innocence and genuine love which La felt for Tarzan is somehow lacking in Nemone. Like a cruel and whimsical teenager, her enthusiasms for the apeman wax and wane with the ebb and flow of her precarious grasp on reality.

In the case of La of Opar there is a sense that, circumstances being different, Tarzan might have succumbed to her charms, but not so with Nemone. Tarzan is of course older and more experienced at this point, and sees through her tantrums and erratic behavior, past the external dazzle, to the dark and turbulent emotions that play upon her boredom and need for excitement. His first introduction to her is in the richly appointed audience chamber of the palace:

> her movements seemed to Tarzan a combination of the seductive languor of the sensualist and the sinuous grace and savage alertness of the tigress.
>
> That she was marvellously beautiful by the standards of any land or any time grew more apparent to the lord of the jungle as she came nearer to him, yet her presence exhaled a subtle essence that left him wondering if her beauty were the reflection of a nature all good or all evil, for her mien and bearing suggested that there could be no compromise—Nemone, the Queen, was all one or all the other. (67)

In the event, she turns out to be "all the other," and quite unbalanced in the bargain. Like many of the nobles, she has a passion for the great lions so dear to Cathne's heart, but her passion in particular for the great beast Belthar is perhaps suggestively Ovidian in its histrionic complexity. In a scene of no small emblematic value, she commits suicide at the end of the book by plunging a knife into her breast and falling dead across the corpse of her beloved animal.

Nemone, like Jane and Kala, is at the extreme tip of the spectrum that the females of the novels populate, and the scores who must here remain unmentioned locate themselves at various intervals on that imaginary scale. Many, indeed most, become involved not with Tarzan but with the secondary male characters, often in an implicit kind of triangular relationship in which Tarzan proves to be the excluded member of the trio. Typical is Tarzan's "first love," the she-ape Teeka in *Jungle Tales of Tarzan,* who selects the ape Taug and thus breaks Tarzan's young heart. Only Jane Porter is able likewise to affect Tarzan later in life, before their marriage, and once he and she have undertaken their vows he never seriously wavers. Like that of all true heroes, even his amatory commitment is total and undeviating, and both Jane and Nemone furnish in their opposite ways ample proof of this requisite dimension to the hero's personality

Assessment

There is no denying either the popularity or the longevity of the Tarzan novels. Since the first one was written in 1912, they have gone through numerous editions, and countless copies of each have been sold. It is difficult to establish with quantitative accuracy the true extent of the literary Tarzan's popularity, but reasonable estimates may be extrapolated from a variety of sources.

In his survey of American best-sellers, Frank Mott[10] includes for a given decade those books whose sales had equaled at least one percent of the country's population at the time of the book's publication. For the decade 1910–19 he singles out *Tarzan of the Apes* as one book that, published in 1914 (along with Booth Tarkington's *Penrod* and Harold Bell Wright's *The Eyes of the World*), had at least reached the target figure of 900,000 copies. Other novelists listed by Mott for this period are Florence Barclay, Zane Grey, Edgar Guest, Kathleen Norris, Eleanor H. Porter, and Gene Stratton-Porter.

Q. D. Leavis, who conducted a study in the early thirties of America's sixty most popular writers, considered as subjects those authors who had met one or more of the following criteria: 1) Having written "the Novel of the Season"; 2) being steady bestsellers over a long period; 3) having proportionally larger sales for a given public.[11] She ranks Burroughs among "the great names in popular fiction . . . in the last generation" (54), and comments that his "books sell a million copies a year" (53; cf. 55). Before appending her list of the most popular works for 1900–19, she asserts that each novel is "representative of popular fiction of its time, and if a gap in years is left it may be assumed that the same kind of fiction was being read in the interval. In general, the first successful novel only of a steady bestseller is recorded" (330). It is surely significant that no other work is listed until 1919; it was during this period 1914–19, of course, that Burroughs wrote and published the next six works in the Tarzan series. Burroughs's continued popularity is evident not only from the fact that his own name as well as that of his most famous literary creation, Tarzan, are today household words, but also that his works still sell extremely well (see below). Many of the other giants of the period 1900–19, however, among whom Leavis ranked him in the early thirties are today virtual unknowns. These include Florence Barclay, Ethel M. Dell, Gilbert Frankau, Jefferey Farnol, Maurice Hewlett, Robert Hichens, W. J. Locke, Baroness Orczy, H. de Vere Stacpoole and H. A. Vachell.

The fall 1984 edition of *Paperbound Books in Print* lists a total of fifty Burroughs titles in print, of which forty-four are different novels; and *Books in Print 1984–1985* lists a total of seventy-four

Burroughs works in print, of which fifty-five are different titles. It is instructive to compare the figures for the other novelists mentioned above (the pattern "Burroughs 50–44 : 74–55" means fifty total and forty-four different titles in *Paperbound Books in Print* for Fall 1984 and seventy-four total and fifty-five different titles in *Books in Print 1984–1985*): Florence Barclay 0–0 : 0–0; Ethel M. Dell 0–0 : 13–11; Jefferey Farnol 0–0 : 3–3; Gilbert Frankau 0–0 : 1–1; Zane Grey 32–32 : 68–55; Edgar Guest 0–0 : 7–7; Maurice Hewlett 0–0 : 6–6; Robert Hichens 1–1 : 1–1; W. J. Locke 0–0 : 1–1; Kathleen Norris 1–1 : 14–13; Baroness Orczy 2–2 : 4–4; Eleanor H. Porter 0–0 : 6–5; Gene Stratton-Porter 1–1 : 14–11; H. de Vere Stacpoole 0–0 : 1–1; Booth Tarkington 0–0 : 21–14; Horace A. Vachell 0–0 : 1–1; and Harold Bell Wright 0–0 : 1–1. Not one of these writers is in the same category as Burroughs in strict terms of number of volumes still in print, although Zane Grey and, to a lesser extent, Gene Stratton-Porter, and Booth Tarkington have not done too badly themselves. Two other legendary novelists who were contemporaries of Burroughs and not captured in the above lists also merit notice here: Mary Roberts Rinehart and H. G. Wells. Their publication figures are, respectively, 3–2 : 17–15 and 31–16 : 10–10, which rank them with Grey and Tarkington but far below Burroughs in current popularity.

By 1947 Mott could state that "Edgar Rice Burroughs, Inc. estimates *Tarzan of the Apes* has exceeded five million the world over and has reached a million and a half or more in the United States. Perhaps four or five times those amounts would give the grand totals for all the Tarzan books."[12] This amounts to some 20 to 25 million[13] copies by 1947—for the Tarzan series alone.[14] Given publishers' notorious secrecy regarding publication figures, it is impossible to do anything but guess at the total of all the Burroughs novels sold by the end of World War II, but it must have been considerable, to say the least. The estimate of Alice Hackett[15] is somewhat more restrained than those disclosed above, for she suggests that by the end of 1965 some 750,000 hardbound copies of *Tarzan of the Apes* had been sold.

The fact that Burroughs does not appear on lists compiled by Irving Harlow Hart for *Publisher's Weekly* during the first half of this century is not an argument against his continuing popularity, for in contrast to the authorities mentioned above, Hart based his lists not necessarily on numbers but "followed a system of his own in determining the scores of books and authors."[16] Since this system is not explained, his results may be viewed as open to some question. Hart furthermore appears only to have considered an author for the year in which a given work was published, for no "account is taken of the continued popularity of books and authors through reprints."[17]

Although publication of the novels waned during World War II, they continued to be sold for about another decade. The fifties and early sixties were a period of commercial inactivity for the Burroughs works. In 1961 only nine (hardback) Tarzan novels were listed as in print on a backlist of Grosset & Dunlap.[18] And the 1962 issue of *Paperbound Books in Print* lists only one Burroughs work in print, a collection entitled *The Martian Novels* and consisting of *Thuvia, Maid of Mars, Chessmen of Mars,* and *Mastermind of Mars,* put out by Dover.

By 1965, however, a radical change had taken place,[19] for as Paul Mandel notes the "Tarzan books, along with other works of their author, Edgar Rice Burroughs, are runaway bestsellers today [i.e., 1963] and have been ever since they began to come out last year. They have sold something more than 10 million copies, almost one thirtieth the total annual sales of all paperbacks in the U.S." (11). The February 1965 issue of *Paperbound Books in Print* lists a total of seventy-six Burroughs works in print, some of which were duplicate editions being put out by several different publishers. Twenty years later, the fall 1984 edition of *Paperbound Books in Print* lists, as we saw above, a total of forty-four different Burroughs titles in print, and *Books in Print 1984–1985* registers fifty-five different novels in print. A comparable scale of publishing activity during the last generation is also in evidence in the United Kingdom, as is made clear from consultation of *Paperbacks in Print.* As for the non-English output of Burroughs's novels, it is simply impossible to say, especially in the case of Russia (where Tarzan has long been very popular),[20] which does not recognize International Copyright conventions.

We can reasonably conclude, then, that the fact of Burroughs's continued popularity (with the exception of some ten years in the fifties and early sixties), sustained over a period of almost four generations, is neither fad nor subject to serious debate.

Burroughs got his start writing for the pulps, and the attempt

to locate him among the more important pulp writers is therefore
an appropriate exercise.

The pulps themselves were an outgrowth of the most remarkable
phenomenon in the history of American publishing, the dime novel.
First introduced in 1860, the dime novel held sway as mass entertainment for the next fifty years until it was effectively replaced by
the pulp magazines, the first of which was Frank Munsey's *Argosy*
put out in 1896. Burroughs began to publish just as the dime novel
was dying and the pulp magazines were coming into their maturity.
Like many of his generation, Burroughs must have read his share
of dime novels, of which it has been estimated[21] that some 7500
different titles were published. In a fifty-year period this amounts
to approximately 150 a year, or about one every three days for half
a century. One writer alone, the indefatigable Horatio Alger, is said
(Bleiler, page vii) to have sold over a quarter billion copies of his
works, and this at a time when the nation's population was well
below 100 million. Although the quality of the dime novels appears
to have been questionable,[22] during "the years of its heyday . . .
the dime novel permeated young America, molding folkways in the
same manner that television does today" (Bleiler, page ix). As was
to be the case with the later pulps, the dime novel fell into various
categories, such as detective, science fiction and "invention" stories,
frontier adventure and, in a later development, self-improvement.
Indeed, Bleiler indicates that the decades of the 1860s and 1870s
were largely given over to an obsession with the frontier and the
West, the 1880s and 1890s to crime and detection, and the last
phase of the phenomenon to self-improvement and the betterment
of one's status in society (the familiar Horatio Alger theme). It is
thus clear that a huge popular demand had already been in place
for several generations when the pulps came on the scene. The demise
of the dime novel has been traced to the prohibitive cost that a raise
in the postal rates forced onto the publishers, as well as the more
sophisticated appeal of the emergent pulps, which spoke to adults
as well as adolescents.

The most immediate appeal of Burroughs's first pulp fiction,
Under the Moons of Mars (published by Robert H. Davis of *All Story*
in 1912, and later becoming the novel *A Princess of Mars*, first of
the initial Martian trilogy), was its innovative (at the time) combination of contemporary canons of popular science fiction and "invention" literature with a strong romantic component. This was the

so-called space opera, or science-fiction romance. And from the very start Burroughs was enormously popular with readers. Henry Steeger, founder and president of Popular Publications, Inc. (which at one point was publishing up to almost fifty different pulps every month), mentions Edgar Rice Burroughs as one of the outstanding successes in pulp writing.[23] It is worthwhile to look at Burroughs in the context of other hugely popular pulp writers of the day in the same way that we considered the best-selling authors above. Indeed, some of these pulp authors became, like Burroughs, bestselling authors in their own right in later years; and some of these are, again like Burroughs, still read by large audiences in the middle and late 1980s.

Steeger's list (Goodstone, page v), then, with publication format the same as for the novelists mentioned earlier, is the following: Max Brand [Frederick Faust] 53–53 : 100–77; Lord Buchnan 0–0 : 0–0; C. S. Forester 15–13 : 36–26; Erle Stanley Gardner 16–16 : 52–44; Harold Lamb 2–2 : 0–0; Talbot Mundy 5–5 : 9–6; Leonard Nason 0–0 : 0–0; Frank Packard 0–0 : 2–2; Tod Robbins 0–0 : 0–0; and Sax Rohmer 1–1 : 22–21. Compared to Burroughs's figures of 50–44 : 74–55, only Max Brand surpasses him in statistical popularity, although Erle Stanley Gardner probably outdid them both (if one considers the many pseudonyms under which he wrote). Although hundreds if not thousands eked out a living in the "pulp jungle,"[24] few, it appears, made it big in the long run. To what can the durability of a Max Brand, an Edgar Rice Burroughs, or an Erle Stanley Gardner be attributed?

Each of these authors had their original pulp work put out in novel form relatively soon after initial publication, and this certainly helped to preserve them beyond the ephemeral life cycle of the fugitive pulp magazines. Each was also in his own way an innovator of genres that had a solid foundation in the dime novels of the late nineteenth century. Where Burroughs altered the trend in science fiction and adventure romance, Gardner built his reputation with the detective story[25] and Max Brand changed the "realistic" Westerns of the Zane Grey school into tales with a vigorously mythic dimension.[26]

As we have seen above, Burroughs was but one of countless writers feeding the voracious hungers of the average reader. The kinds of analyses that have been offered in the previous pages are to some extent applicable to other authors who were mining the same general lode of mass readership at which Burroughs was busy. Yet not many are known today even by name, much less still extant. Burroughs's Tarzan, however, continues to confound the detractors and still enjoys huge success in the marketplace. This is all the more remarkable, given the vastly greater number of authors and books that compete for readers' attention now compared to sixty or seventy years ago.

We are thus faced with something of a quandary, the attempt to describe with any degree of exactitude what it is about the Tarzan stories that has continued and still continues to fascinate to such an extraordinary degree. Nor is it clear that the dilemma is, in all honesty, resolvable. It would be facile and less than disingenuous to appeal to the demonstrably mythic structure of these stories as the explanation, for many contemporary tales were also mythic in design. Stylistic criteria are not very helpful here either, for although Burroughs was not the grammatical and linguistic hack that critics (and, at times, he himself) have so often asserted, other writers who have not survived on any comparable scale were certainly no less capable in their handling of the language. As for the element of fantasy and imagination, it must be admitted that Burroughs was extraordinarily inventive, but so were other, even more "mainline" authors like Jules Verne or H. G. Wells, and though popular, their works have never enjoyed anything like the sustained and truly astonishing popularity of Tarzan.

Invocation of external factors as explanatory criteria is not much more helpful. Thus, Burroughs was a shrewd purveyor of his writings in his own lifetime, and his heirs in the Edgar Rice Burroughs Corporation are no less astute in marketing their product. But even the slickest marketing in the world will not sell what the public does not want, and surely not for so many years. And although the movies and television series featuring Tarzan have certainly kept the name in the public mind, most viewers are not even aware that the novels exist; and furthermore, the one-dimensionality and outright silliness of the cinematic translations would not hold great appeal to those who know their Tarzan from the books. It may of course be that some movie-goers have subsequently sought out the books, but these are surely in the minority.

What can we say, then, in conclusion to our discussion of the Tarzan novels and their ubiquitous attractiveness? A frank answer must entertain the likelihood of its own elusiveness in attempting to explicate the success of this literary personality. We can address Burroughs's not inconsiderable mastery of style and the cliff-hanging narrative pace; we can with justification point to the pervasive mythic underpinning; and we can speak of the author's enormous capacity for invention—and yet fail to capture an essential explanation for the durability of the hero.

Two suggestions present themselves: the novels' role as unabashed wish-fulfillment and the protagonist's character as missing link.

All fiction of the type "romance" caters axiomatically to individuals' fantasies of love, power, and wealth, and the Tarzan stories are no exception. Tarzan is above all an individual who has full mastery of his destiny, and on those occasions when a situation does get out of control he is able to face it with equanimity and (to use a very modern term) total "cool." Tarzan's appeal may lie in part in his capacity to direct and even shape events of the most negative sort in such a fashion that they ultimately work for instead of against him. His ability to slice through the tough bias of organizational complexities (be they those of jungle societies, lost civilizations, religious institutions, or modern Paris) to the bone of problems and difficulties is surely an appealing if recognizably unreal quality in a hero. In Tarzan's literary persona such abilities redress vicariously the generalized sense of powerlessness and lack of personal control that seem to characterize self-perceptions in the increasingly hierarchical world of the late twentieth century. His low-keyed indifference to the consequences of violating often meaningless codes enshrined in a society's system of values speaks with eloquence to the iconoclastic impulse of readers in any age. We would all on occasion like to have that kind of self-assurance and control, and Tarzan's embodiment of it may well offer partial justification for our fascination with him.

On a different level, Tarzan comes close to being the most perfectly realized version of the "missing link," the ultimate connection between our human selves and our animal ancestors. Of course, the sharply delineated Darwinism (however "popularized" its form may be) of the entire Tarzan mythos implicitly invites such a comparison. New discoveries in Africa and elsewhere about the origins of mankind and our relationship to hominid ancestors occupying some evolutionary rung that is neither true simian nor true human attest to our deeply rooted interest in our own ultimate provenience. Given the circumstances of Tarzan's birth and upbringing, as well as his bridging the worlds of jungle and civilization, it hardly seems overly bold to suggest that he has come to occupy a niche in the popular fancy as a kind of emblematic representative of our own origins.

Chapter Five
Minor Cycles:
Pellucidar and Venus

Over the thirty-five years of his creative career Burroughs wrote several interconnected works, or cycles, besides those featuring Tarzan and John Carter. Since full discussion of all of them would not substantially alter the critical view of his contribution to popular literature, two of the best-known[1] (Pellucidar and Venus), and a few miscellaneous works, are here selected for comment.

Pellucidar

From the start of his writing career Burroughs was taken with the old idea that a counterworld existed at the center of our own earth. Although he certainly did not invent the notion,[2] he worked with it in a series of "inner-world" novels beginning with *At the Earth's Core* in 1913, including the thirteenth Tarzan novel (*Tarzan at the Earth's Core* [1928 −29]), and ending with *Savage Pellucidar* (1940–44). Others in the series are *Pellucidar* (1914), *Tanar of Pellucidar* (1928), *Back to the Stone Age* (1935), and *Land of Terror* (1938–39).

Early Pellucidar. The first one in the group, *At the Earth's Core* recounts in a framing structure the tale of David Innes's and Abner Perry's marvelous journey in their giant borer into the interior of the earth. Innes is, down to his gray eyes and startling physique, a Tarzan-type, and the story bears all the hallmarks of Burroughs's narrative embellishments and social criticism: the effeteness of modern civilization, the workings of generations of evolutionary development to produce modern man, and the triangular love story with its misunderstandings, heroic rescues, evil monsters, and love triumphant. The book is also strong on manifest destiny, for Innes, who becomes emperor-leader of a collection of tribes in the inner world (aptly named Pellucidar from its eternal sunlight), federalizes the various groups along lines strongly suggestive of our own form of government. This Americanization of Pellucidar no doubt reflects American zeal in general for bringing its version of civilization to others. Coupled with Innes's more secular approach is the religious justification that Perry provides:

I believe that God sent us here for just that purpose—it shall be my life work to teach them His word—to lead them into the light of His mercy while we are training their hearts and hands in the ways of culture and civilization. (72)

Although such action no longer enjoys quite the same vogue in a post–World War II and post–Vietnam era, we must recall that Burroughs was a Teddy Roosevelt Republican and that in 1913 the culturally ethnocentric dogmas of manifest destiny were socially accepted and even a national policy, as they have been until relatively recent times.

A curious paradox emerges from a consideration of the conceptual underpinning of this novel. As an anti-world, Burroughs treats it in many ways as a prism through which are refracted institutions and practices on earth, to the detriment of the latter. Thus, where earth has water, Pellucidar has land, and vice versa (65f.), and this topographical antithesis parallels more interesting cultural antitheses. This world has developed along different evolutionary lines, and where earth holds reptiles in lowest esteem, in Pellucidar they are the ruling race. These Mahars, as they are called, indulge in practices that from the earthman's perspective are repugnant, but in fact are no different from what earthmen do vis-a-vis other living things that they, earthmen, consider inferior to themselves. And since mankind has progressed only to a Stone Age level in Pellucidar and are deemed of an inferior status by the Mahars, their treatment (which includes vivisection by Mahar scientists) by the Mahars is quite logical. As Perry says to David:

What is there horrible about it, David? They understand us no better than we understand the lower animals of our own world. Why, I have come across here very learned discussions of the question as to whether *gilaks,* that is men, have any means of communication. . . . Because we do not converse as they do it is beyond them to imagine that we converse at all. It is thus that we reason in relation to the brutes of our own world. . . . (69).

The narrative aspects of *At the Earth's Core* are pure Burroughs. Innes, the hero, falls in love with the primitive Dian the Beautiful, and sets off on a long quest in search of her after an abduction. On the way he makes friends with local primitives, fights gorillalike savages and a host of paleontological monsters, endures capture and makes escapes, and is finally reunited and married with Dian. The amatory element in the story is spiced up with the usual triangular complications (e.g., Jubal the Ugly and Hooja the Sly One), and Dian herself proves to be of royal blood among the tribe of Amoz, over whom her brother Dacor the Strong rules. The story moves at a swift pace, but is predictable; its general shape was to be recast on numerous occasions in subsequent stories featuring Tarzan, John Carter, Carson Napier, and others. In 1913 it was still fresh, but readers coming to it after the major works will find little of novelty.

Burroughs ends the story in such a way that a sequel must follow: like Tarzan at the end of *Tarzan of the Apes* and John Carter at the end of *A Princess of Mars,* so too David Innes at the end of his first tale is separated from his beloved, and it is unclear if the two shall ever again be reunited.

The second book in the "inner world" series, *Pellucidar,* offers, again, little of novelty in comparison with the first. The hero, David Innes, has returned to earth to acquire various materials and technological support so that he and Perry can realize their goal of bringing the civilization of the outer crust to the relatively primitive interior. His grandiose schemes for civilizing an entire primitive world sounds remarkably like the kind of program the French and British pursued in Africa in the late nineteenth and early twentieth centuries, as well as elsewhere (e.g., India {British} and Viet Nam {French}). There is in Innes's mind, as in the minds of the political leaders of the Europe of the day, no serious doubt about the worthwhileness of imposing foreign customs and social institutions on unasking natives. Consider Innes's observations at the end of the novel:

Before we sailed I went to Gr-gr-gr, chief of the beast-men, taking Juag with me. There the three of us arranged a code of laws that would permit the brute-folk and human beings of the island to live in peace and harmony. Gr-gr-gr sent his son with me back to Sari, capital of my empire, that he might learn the ways of human beings. I have hopes of turning this race into the greatest agriculturists of Pellucidar. (177)

And somewhat later:

> I think that by teaching him to read and write English we shall then be able more quickly to give them a written language of their own.
> And this was the nucleus about which we were to build our great system of schools and colleges. (184)

It is in this sense that Burroughs is most self-evidently a child of his age. If we can today with hindsight criticize his ready acceptance of such national Pygmalion-complexes, we do well to recall at the same time that he was not unaware of the possibly adverse consequences of such policies. Thus, in the same novel, Innes speaks also against certain aspects of the colonial model, as emerges from his chastisement of Perry:

> I said that we must give them the best we have. What we have given them so far has been the worst. We have given them war and the munitions of war. In a single day we have made their wars infinitely more terrible and bloody than in all their past ages they have been able to make them with their crude, primitive weapons. (175)

The novel, like the whole Pellucidarian cycle, is a kind of utopian vision,[3] with the American David Innes providing the moral and military leadership necessary to create Western order out of primitive chaos.[4] Its ending is as harmonious and restful as that of the previous novel was disconcerting and filled with uncertainty. Like the second Tarzan novel *(Return of Tarzan)*, the second Pellucidar novel dispells the disequilibrium of the first in the series, and the reader is meant to sense that the program of Innes, with his empress Dian, and Perry is now about to begin. During the endless searching, capture by various primitives, and escape, repeated time after time, we have been taken on a kind of ethnographic and topographic[5] survey of this new world, and thus have a strong sense of the majesty which the author wished to impute to Innes's grand undertaking as culture hero par excellence.

   The middle period.   The third book of the Pellucidar series, *Tanar of Pellucidar,* follows a general pattern observed in both the Tarzan and John Carter series: shifting the focus from the protagonist to a younger person of the following generation. Thus, *The Son of Tarzan* is essentially a Tarzan novel featuring the Tarzan-like son of the apeman, and *Thuvia, Maid of Mars* is about Carthoris, the son of John Carter and his princess, Dejah Thoris. Tanar of Pellucidar is the son of Ghak, one of the first native rulers in Pellucidar to support David Innes in his establishment of the Federated Kingdoms of Pellucidar, and this book recounts the adventures he experienced while on an abortive rescue. Captured by the piratelike Korsars who ply the seas of inner earth, he falls in love with Stellara, the daughter of The Cid, leader of these cruel pillagers. Tanar's tale is standard fare, replete with peevishly stubborn heroine, love triangles, marauding rivals for erotic affections, shameless coincidence and chance meetings, unceasing alternations of· capture, escape or rescue, and recapture. It is perhaps fair to suggest that Tanar is simply a stone-age Tarzan translated from the jungles of Africa to the jungles of Pellucidar. It is surely no coincidence that the one "cross-over" Tarzan novel[6] was written at this period, nor that Tanar's very name is remarkably close to Tarzan's. As warmed-over apeman, however, *Tanar of Pellucidar* is tiresomely repetitive and predictable. But there is one sequence in the book that is of interest for the possible shadow it casts of events in Burroughs's personal life at the time.

In the course of Tanar's extensive wanderings and captivities in Pellucidar the reader is taken, as so often, on ethnographic excursions. Thus, one of the peoples among whom he spends time are the strange Himeans. Here he is befriended by the young woman Gura (one of several mistaken rivals with Stellara for his love), who explains the bizarre family life of her people. It consists of constant bickering and physical abuse of all family members by each other. In graphic antithesis to the smoothly harmonious social life of the island of love, Amiocap,[7] the world of the Himeans is all bitter family life. As Gura explains:

They take their mates for life and are permitted but one and though both men and women have a choice in the selection of their mates they never seem to be satisfied with one another and are always quarreling, usually because neither one nor the other is faithful. Do the men and women quarrel thus in the land from which you come? (160)

It is worth noting that at the time (1928) of the writing of *Tanar of Pellucidar* Burroughs's own marriage to Emma was showing unmistakable signs of the strain that was to eventuate in divorce a few years later (in 1934 [*ERB,* passim]).

Deterioration.   The next to the last novel, *Land of Terror,* was written in the period 1938–39. It displays the creaking signs of a narrative formula worked to exhaustion. The plot is all too familiar by now: capture, a new community, escape, romantic entanglements and threats to the woman in question, the meeting of a fellow prisoner, more escapes and captures, the endless trekking across lost worlds on searches for missing women and friends.

This particular novel almost seems to go out of its way to be puerile, and the sexism is at times astonishing. Thus, at the start of the story, David Innes is taken captive by a brutal group of Amazonian women, about whom he reflects that if

these women were the result of taking women out of slavery and attempting to raise them to equality with man, then I think that they and the world would be better off if they were returned to slavery. One of the sexes must rule; and man seems temperamentally better fitted for the job than woman. Certainly if full power over man has resulted in debauching and brutalizing women to such an extent, then we should see that they remain always subservient to man, whose overlordship is, more often than not, tempered by gentleness and sympathy. (21–22)

The novel continues in a strictly linear fashion, one meaningless event following on another; the emphasis is exclusively on action. It is unfortunate that the series should have deteriorated so noticeably, for it was not without interest in its earlier episodes. However, a period of some twenty-five years had elapsed since the first Pellucidar work appeared, and the torrent of words that had poured forth from Burroughs's pen in the interim had clearly drained him of the original verve and liveliness. This is, unhappily, Burroughs's action-plotting at its thinnest and most unsatisfying. There is nothing but sheer narrative pulse to propel the reader onward, and the journey is one through numbingly familiar terrain. Possibly one of Burroughs's worst novels, *Land of Terror* is almost a self-parody, tired and enervated, going through the narrative motions and arriving nowhere. The book ends with one of those incredible coincidences that gathers together all the loose strands into an unusually adventitious resolution of standardized sort: the rejoining of David and Dian, and the marriage of a couple and the next generation on the way.

In the last of the Pellucidar series, *Savage Pellucidar,* a pervasive sense of déjà vu dominates. Written in four sections (three in 1940 and one in 1944), the book is ostensibly about the wanderings of David Innes and his wife, Dian the Beautiful, in their eternal search-and-rescue of each other. The plot concentrates on David's emissary, Hodon the Fleet One, and his beloved, O-aa of Kali, but the names hardly matter anymore, for this is fiction at its worst. The thematic concerns have by this time an anesthetizing familiarity about them: the love triangle, superstition and religious quackery, capture-escape-capture and escape-capture-escape, and the barbed asides about the meaning of civilization as it was brought to Pellucidar by Perry and his inventions of war. A kind of comic relief is meant to be provided by this impractical worthy, and he is relief indeed next to the mindlessly conceived character of the Old Man from New England. The latter, some 150 years old, came by mistake to Pellucidar many generations ago. It is difficult to discern just what the point of his role is within the larger economy of the narrative; perhaps he is nothing but an auctorial reflex interwoven into the loose strands of the finished fabric. In 1944 Burroughs was one year shy of seventy, and he had been writing these stories for over thirty years. They did not get better with age.

Savage Pellucidar, being among the very last complete works Burroughs wrote, makes for an unhappy conclusion to an ambitious writing career.

Venus

The five novels that constitute the Venus (also called Amtor) series *(Pirates of Venus* [1931], *Lost on Venus* [1932], *Carson of Venus* [1937], *Escape on Venus* [1940], and *The Wizard of Venus* [1941]) were written relatively late in Burroughs's life. They display the weary signs of a genre that has grown tired and a hero whose personality and actions border at times on self-caricature. For the protagonist of this cycle, Carson Napier of Virginia, is almost pure stereotype and embarrassingly lacking in any of the individual interest even of a John Carter or, especially, Tarzan. A kind critic has said of the books, "In *The Wizard of Venus* Burroughs was beginning to break new ground in a series previously rather dull; it is a pity that he did not go on to develop the Amtorian sequence with newer and more imaginative ideas than those in the earlier books."[8] A similar observation is recorded by Brian V. Aldiss, who comments that "although generously supplied with strange topography, people and adventures, [Venus] never has quite the zip of the Martian series."[9]

Narrative design. A typical plot unfolds as follows. The hero arrives, usually in unwitting or unwilling fashion, in a marvelously strange land, which may be essentially hostile, like that of the Amazons at the beginning of *Carson of Venus,* or benign, as in the case of his initial descent to Venus and the households of Mintep and Duran in *Pirates of Venus.* Initially suspect, he is put to some kind of test, which may have been created as a genuine touchstone of his worthiness to be incorporated into the society, or as a thinly disguised means to permanent expulsion through death. The latter kind of testing is best exemplified by the predicament in which the hero is placed at the start of *Lost on Venus.* Here he is abandoned in the chilling Room of Seven Doors, all the more terrifying for the psychological as well as the physical anguish which it is designed to evoke in its victims. Next the hero either escapes from captors, as from the cruel Myposans in *Escape on Venus,* or is captured by monstrous enemies while on some errand for, or in the company of, new-found friends. The abduction by the birdmen in *Pirates of Venus* while he is hunting tarel with his friend Kamlot is a good case in point.

A primary quest throughout the series is the ongoing search for Duare, princess of Vepaja, who alternately is with the hero or has been carried off by savage foemen. Her coy indecisiveness plays constant foil to the hero's amatory assertiveness, and erotic unions with repulsive monsters of varied hue and stripe are imminent but never to be consummated (e.g., the brute raiders in the garden in *Pirates of Venus,* the necrophiliac Skor of Kormor in *Lost on Venus,* the animalistic Tyros in *Escape on Venus,* and so forth).

Central to many of the plots, as well as subplots, is the theme of political revolution brought on by or promoting social and moral corruption, which may be either material (as with the Zanis in *Carson of Venus*) or spiritual and intellectual (as with the grisly eugenics of the utopian Havatooans in *Lost on Venus*). The hero not infrequently takes it upon himself, or is thrust by circumstances, to become both theoretician and soldier in the inevitable counter-revolutionary overthrow of incumbent evil. This almost demagogic assumption of power is evident on the microcosmic scale of subplot, as in the mutiny in *Pirates of Venus* against their Thorist officers by incensed rowers and underlings who have been fueled with the hero's smoldering outrage; it shows up also in the kaleidoscope of shifting intrigues among the peoples of Mypos, Japal, Panga, Falsa, and Hangor in *Escape on Venus*. And interspersed amid these violent upheavals are numerous minor captures and escapes, bizarre forms of imprisonment, and complicating erotic triangles.

It is not unusual for the hero in some way toward the end of a tale sequence to show himself responsible for effecting a purging change in the local government or helping an erstwhile exile to restore himself as citizen or ruler. In the conclusion to the warlike events charted in *Carson of Venus*, for example, Taman's establishment as leader of Sanara is chiefly the consequence of Carson's ingenuity and initiative; and in *Escape on Venus*, at the end of the revolutionary machinations within Japal, Kandar wins the ruling power largely through the moral and material support of Carson Napier.

In counterpoint to this sense of resolution in the world at large we may find an element of personal disequilibrium in the disappearance of the hero from the newly reintegrated society. At the conclusion to *Escape on Venus*, for example, various individuals are restored to the groups from which they have been in exile, but the hero vanishes with his friend Ero Shan and princess Duare into the mountains, still not yet a part of a larger social order.

The standard story-line[10] of a Venus-tale, then, consists of the hero's going astray or losing himself at the beginning; encountering a number of helpful and harmful individuals or groups either in the general course of his wanderings or in the quest for a missing woman or friend; and, after helping to re-create order out of political chaos, himself continuing his journey.

This schematic description of the general tale structure reveals similarities to the very common patterning of the wandering hero made famous long ago by Homer in the *Odyssey* and Vergil in the *Aeneid*. For the protagonist in each of these notable epics is essentially a wanderer, searching as much for himself as he is for home, whether an old (as does Odysseus) or a new one (as does Aeneas). Each meets in the course of his travels strange humans and stranger monsters, encounters tricky amatory situations, and undertakes a journey into the lower world. But the similarity, for all its compelling allure, is superficial, restricted to the mere pattern of endless wandering interspersed with dangerous escapades. For Carson as characterized persona is among the thinnest of Burroughs's creations: unlike an

Odysseus or Aeneas, he never changes, never learns, never grows, never questions, never, it seems, has time to think about anything except how to find Duare or extricate himself from his latest folly.

Modularity of composition. Modular composition, or formula writing, has assumed shameless proportions in the Venus books. It is not that use of literary pattern is inherently objectionable, for paradigms may be employed to create expectations that are then subjected to ironic reversal.

In Homer's *Odyssey,* for example, the formulaic scene in which guests are welcomed by a genial and civilized host, feted, and sent on their way, is repeated several times in the opening books of the poem. The iterated sequence in effect establishes what is appropriate behavior in that heroic world between host and guest. When, therefore, in book 9 the hero and his men come to the cave of the monster Polyphemus, the latter subverts the established expectation of the formula and, instead of giving his guests food to eat, eats his guests. The inversion thus underscores the uncivilized and monstrous behavior of Polyphemus. The pattern is made to work for the author, and is not simply a slothful shorthand. Similarly, later in the epic when Odysseus slays the suitors who are guests in his home, it is clear that because the suitors have violated what has been established earlier in the poem as proper behavior of guests, Odysseus is, by the code of that society, justified in actions that otherwise might have seemed quite shocking.

Although Burroughs follows the outward form of such traditional means of composition, a strategy for their organic incorporation into the stories quite escapes him here.[11] Consider the general formulation of such a scene, the hero's stereotypical encounter with an animal monster in *Pirates of Venus:*

Suddenly, above me, to the crashing of some heavy body through the foliage were added hideous screams and snarls; and in the terrifying dissonance I recognized the presence of more than a single creature. . . . Looking up quickly, I saw a creature launching itself toward me and just beyond it a snarling face of utter hideousness. I caught but the briefest glimpse of it—just enough to see that it was a face, with eyes and a mouth. . . . I saw confronting me a creature that might be conjured only in the half-delerium of some horrid nightmare . . . two more spears, hurled by the companions of the first man, drove into his chest, and with a last frightful scream, the thing dropped dead. (40–46)

At first the hero (or heroine) is made aware of imminent danger by the acoustic signals emitted by the lurking beast, and such vocabulary as "noise," "scream," "snarl," and "din" occurs with predictable frequency. This very language of the sound that the attacker makes becomes a kind of subliminal cue that precisely such a scene is being initiated. Once the auditory embellishments have been described, the visual horror of the strange creature is depicted, often in great detail. The hero's effort to save himself and the subsequent combat with the beast constitute the core of the action, and these motifs lend themselves naturally to an almost infinite set of variations. Not uncommonly the protagonist is aided by the timely intercession of stranger or friend, and often finds it necessary to draw upon cunning in order to overcome physically superior foes. Feral force is overcome by cool cleverness.

Very briefly, then, the formula on which this type of scene is based entails: 1) noise, 2) description, 3) attack, 4) counterattack, 5) escape or rescue, 6) use of cunning, and 7) help from friend or stranger (including another beast).[12] Such formulaic writing, the structural backbone of popular literature, is at once inordinately confining and potentially liberating. It is as though the author were freed of all need to give serious thought to constructing the mold and hence were at liberty to devote his attention to the material with which the mold is to be filled, or to manipulating the expectations engendered by the formula. It is to Burroughs's debit in this series that he never seems able to rise above the purely mechanical aspects of the formula-as-digest and fashion of it an integrated member of the narrative corpus.

Suffice it to say that we have examined only one subtype of one type of modular passage, the battle against animal opponents. There are other kinds of battle scenes, such as the fight against an evil abductor of a woman, sadistic overseer, a brutal tyrant, and theriomorphic adversaries, to note a few; and there are other types besides battle scenes, such as captures, escapes, erotic entanglements, revolutions, wanderings, betrayals, and many more. Regrettably, the Venus series reveals a tired Burroughs; it is made up of books too palpably formulaic but never exploiting the formulas, novels lacking both narrative and thematic novelty.

Characterization.   Carson Napier, as traditional wanderer, journeys across the mist-shrouded planet Venus to the cities of men, learning of their varied customs and confronting a countless series of evil monsters. At heart a cheerfully unthinking optimist, he is not given over to the periodic brooding and self-contemplative inwardness of a Tarzan; nor, in turn, is he as intimately incorporated into his adopted civilization on Venus as John Carter is on Barsoom. Carson somehow never settles down, never finds whatever it is he so unflaggingly searches for, indeed, never fully materializes from the author's pen as a personality of any depth or genuine interest. At the ending of the last novel, *The Wizard of Venus*, the suggestion that Carson and Ero Shan return to Sanara and its reasonably regular life is just that, a suggestion. It is never realized, and thus the conclusion of the series instills the impression that Carson's future will continue with the same directionless openendedness that has characterized his whole career.

Yet, paradoxically, this last novel does begin to develop Carson into something like a character for whom the reader could muster some enthusiasm. Sadly, Burroughs never gets things to mesh with conviction. This brief tale of some eighty-six pages boldly portrays the hero's intellectual and even mystical powers, which are the only means for crushing Morgas, the evil wizard. This novella parts company with the first four works in the series in that the hero's activity is almost exclusively mental rather than physical. Conjuring up strong intimations of medieval romance, it takes the hero beyond himself, as it were, and makes him a magician with powers even greater than those of Morgas. Perhaps the very idea of a hero so totally reliant on mental prowess is something of a contradiction in terms for a genre so bound to merely depicting one action serially attached to another. For despite the initial promise, the discontinuity in characterization makes this final story perhaps the least successful of the lot.

It is true that Carson has a very scientific bent (witness the building of the rocket) and great curiosity (the wish to ascertain the habitability of Mars [*Pirates of Venus*, 14]), but his interests are essentially extroverted. There is little of the philosophical questioning or ontological speculation to which Tarzan is prone, as in *Jungle Tales of Tarzan*, for example. And, as we have seen, when the nonphysical facet of Carson's personality is featured, as in *The Wizard of Venus*, it assumes an aura of mysticism (no doubt a legacy of his Indian tutor Chand Kabi [cf. *Pirates of Venus*, 13]) and magic directed outward, but none of interest in his own interior geography.

Like the hero, the heroine is not a forcefully articulated character in the Venus series. For Duare, daughter of Mintep, jong of Vepaja, is very much present throughout the novels, whether in actual fact or as remote object of Carson's quest, but she never comes into her own as a credible personality. She is certainly not of comparable vividness with Tarzan's Jane Porter.

Duare, as well as the other major female figure in the novels, Nalte of Andoo, does have certain characteristics in common with other Burroughs heroines. Although they all are subject to constant abduction, threats of being raped, and unstinting hardship, they are not helpless female victims by any means. They share a common spunkiness and at times even save their men from destruction by timely intervention.

The central role of these and other women is as lovers and wives, although no explicit sexual references are ever found. The language is at times too courtly for modern tastes, and the sensibilities still too rooted in Victorian notions of public propriety, but there can be no mistaking the nature of the relationship. Nor does ambiguity attach to the none-too-murky intents of villains toward Duare. The Myposan ruler Tyros seizes Duare quite unceremoniously and makes off with her (*Escape on Venus,* 67ff.); the deadly Skor would like to keep Duare as his bride (*Lost on Venus,* 188ff.); and the unpleasant Vik-yor, as well as his even more unpleasant ruler, Vik-vik-vik, each want Duare for his own private purposes. Although the ostensible goal of the hero's wanderings is the search for the woman Duare, she herself is vague in our imagination even after the completion of the series, a somewhat shadowy, ill-defined personality. We know that she is petulant, has a way of changing her mind about her feelings, is capable of fierce jealousy for Carson, has physical courage, and is technically a princess, but aside from her protestations of eternal love and her manifest interest in things mechanical, we can say very little about her. In that sense she is not an unfit mate for the equivalently depicted hero. And the woman Nalte, who becomes the wife of Ero Shan, is an obvious parallel to Duare, indeed is a principal in the parallel love plot running throughout *Lost on Venus* (see page 224), in which Nalte plays Duare to Ero Shan's Carson.

There are of course other females in these books, but they are sketched in even fuzzier lines. Taman's daughter Naa, abducted by Muso, occupies center stage a brief moment in *Carson of Venus* (16), and acquits herself with a cool resourcefulness. The sexually inverted society of the Amazons constitutes little more than another version of the social experimentation so prevalent in the various cities that Carson visits (*Carson of Venus*, 12ff.), and the unhappy Skabra, wife of Tyros, merely provides a third leg on yet another erotic triangle (*Escape on Venus*, 59). Finally, the peculiar, perhaps deranged, young lady named Vanaja in *The Wizard of Venus* has little if any personality of her own, and seems to function essentially as a "module," that is, as the woman whom the hero must rescue.

The only individuals who evoke any interest in this gallery of insipidness are the mysterious intriguer Zerka in the land of the Zanis (in *Carson of Venus*), and the indolent and inexplicable Loto-El-Ho-Ganja, alias Betty Calwell of Brooklyn, N.Y. (in *Escape on Venus*). Zerka in particular is well drawn by Burroughs as a believable and sympathetic character. She is depicted throughout as totally courageous and decent, a woman of breeding and intelligence, filled with deep animosity over the status to which her country has been reduced, and one willing to take enormous risks in order to achieve personal and political goals. She is a heroic individual in her own right, and is in fact more interestingly developed as a personality than even Carson—this despite the fact that she appears in only the one book, *Carson of Venus*.

Situated at opposite poles of the spectrum these two women, Loto-El-Ho-Ganja in the direction of lotophagic passivity and mysticism, Zerka in that of the concrete present and committed engagement, are genuine characters to which no other individuals in this series can measure up.

General comments. Although Carson Napier of Venus is one of the last new creations of Burroughs, he does not measure up as hero, nor do his tales as narratives compete with such earlier successes as Tarzan and John Carter of Mars. Somehow, the old magic has tarnished. There are two levels on which it makes sense to try to account for what even dedicated Burroughs-fans would admit are not the crowning achievements of the master's craft.

The predicament is not without its parallel in the history of literature, most notably heroic epic. Both Tarzan and John Carter of Mars move in a literary or mythic universe that only faintly impinges on the real world. True, Tarzan touches base, so to speak, with British aristocracy and Wisconsin hoi polloi, and John Carter has a lineage going far back in Virginia history. It is also true that the author, Burroughs, is mildly intrusive in both sets of tales, functioning, as he does in the Venus series, like an omniscient narrator through whom flows the tale of the hero to the reader: in Tarzan by way of some old documents found in the British Foreign Office (*Tarzan of the Apes,* 1) and an ancient manuscript made accessible to him by an anonymous host; and in the case of John Carter, through the remarkable manuscript that he (Burroughs) was to be allowed to publish only twenty-one years after Carter's death, in 1886 (*A Princess of Mars,* vi–vii). But in both these instances, especially in the earlier works of each series, this traditional framing of the tales by the teller is soon forgotten as we move off into the imaginary landscapes of the African jungle and the dead sea bottoms of the red planet. The narrator remains quite unobtrusively in the background, and the shape of the narratives themselves conforms to the reader's tacit assumptions about the fictional world into which he has been led. The real world impinges very, very little. This is not the case with Carson Napier, and herein lies part of the problem with the series.

Literature as propaganda—even propaganda for "our side"—is at best a problematical undertaking. In particular heroic epic, whose very underpinnings lie in the realms of imagination and fantasy, suffers from mundane intrusions too forcefully reminiscent of the great personalities strutting across the contemporary stage of the real, nonfictional world. A certain reader identification with a hero is essential to a hero's appeal, but if he is too much of this world he is too much like us. It may very well be that some of the later Tarzan novels fail to elicit the excitement of earlier installments in the series precisely because they too become contemporary and place the mythic apeman too often in a world that has too close a connection with the real one and less with the fabulous environment of the jungle.

But it is not merely the politicizing of the one Venus novel in particular (i.e. *Carson of Venus*), with its sharp criticism of European fascism, that accounts for the notable sense of diminished vigor in this series. It is also the way in which Burroughs toys with the literary tradition in which he is working, drawing on it but not doing anything with it. The problems with the Venus novels are as much a result of formal deficiencies as of subject matter generally inappropriate to the genre. Two examples will suffice to illustrate the point, one from *Pirates of Venus* (the storm at the end of the book) and one from *Lost on Venus* (the run-in with Skor in the central section of the book).

Consider the storm sequence first. Carson is sailing back on a captured ship to Vepaja in order to restore Duare to her father's household. At this point a great storm rises up, in the course of which Duare is kidnapped by the birdmen and Carson is swept overboard by a great wave. All but drowning him, the rolling sea offers traditional validation of the hero's interior turbulence and his psychological emersion from the downward pull of the inner personal vortices of spiritual death, despair, and self-doubt. Every hero must endure his "storm," be it Homer's Odysseus, Vergil's Aeneas, or Shakespeare's Lear.

Burroughs dwells at length on this episode, and the physical description of the storm contains some of the most vigorous writing in this novel. It is an unforgettable event, and is sequentially appropriate as a part of the development of the hero at this stage in his career. He is certainly in an emotional turmoil over the ambiguous status of his suit with Duare, so the storm could be read as a type of symbolic statement about traditional heroic themes. In particular, is this "literary" storm a comment about some cleansing change, some escape from a harrowing experience, a final catharsis, a beginning of the reemergence into the normal routines of quotidian existence? It is as though everything points precisely in this direction, and has been set up in this fashion by conscious intent of the author. At the same time, the scene fails utterly to live up to the unmistakable expectations that it has aroused in the reader. For it is surely not the case that Burroughs was unaware of what current literary theory might term the semiotics of the set scene, even if he had never heard it referred to in quite those words. The point is that the larger corpus is filled with masterful examples of just such an awareness and indeed imaginative exploitation of that awareness.[13] Hence it is all the more disappointing to see in these later works merely mechanical deployment of traditional literary icons without any sense of organic articulation with the narrative proper. In short, traditional expectations are created but never allowed to materialize.

A similar charge involves the lengthy entanglement of Carson and Duare with Skor, the ruler in the city of the dead. The presentation of Skor and his habitats points unmistakably to the deity of death and the heroic journey into the underworld, and before

Carson is through with Skor and his city he has undergone as harsh a harrowing of hell as any hero in similar circumstances. Yet, the symbolic import of this descent into hell is rather lost sight of in the novel *(Lost on Venus)*. Carson does rescue his Duare from Skor's clutches, and that is a traditional enough reason for the heroic descent into hell. But there is none of the sense of growth in personal understanding or the larger ways of the external world that so typically are associated with this sequence. Again, Burroughs was most definitely aware of this matter, as is clear from the meticulous way in which it is exploited in *Tarzan and the Jewels of Opar,* for example, or from portions of *Jungle Tales of Tarzan* (e.g., the nocturnal rescue of the moon). In short, he seemed unwilling to flesh out the traditional material in ways that he had done with such masterly ease in the works of a generation earlier.

In conclusion, it may be said that the Venus stories occupy a kind of critical middle ground in the overall evaluation of Burroughs's writings. They are not of the caliber, either substantively or formally, of the Tarzan material or the John Carter series, but nor do they display the silly tendentiousness of, for example, *The Girl from Hollywood.* Their social commentary is as such reasonable enough, but belongs properly not in the unbounded world of fantasy. Americans, one assumes, by and large subscribed to the right to freedom and the pursuit of happiness in the 1930s and 1940s, as they do today, but when a Burroughs hero is too much of the here-and-now and exclaims, with Carson Napier, that he expects to be treated to the "right to life, liberty, and the pursuit of happiness—freedom" *(Pirates of Venus,* 78), he somehow forfeits that status to apartness and specialness that an authentic hero must, it seems, maintain in order to stay timeless.

Miscellaneous Works

It is appropriate to say a word or two about the more obscure items of the Burroughs corpus. These are of two sorts: stand-alone stories that nonetheless are close in conception to the fantasy worlds of the major and minor cycles, and narratives that are localized in the real world, be it a historical period (as with *The Outlaw of Torn*) or contemporary society (as with *The Efficiency Expert*). A few of the second kind are singled out below for brief comment—fuller exposition or more samples can in no way alter in either direction our view of Burroughs as writer.

Social realism.   The early story entitled *The Mucker* (1913) is the first of the few "urban" novels that Burroughs wrote. But even in *The Mucker* Burroughs is soon drawn away from the everyday world of the city to the more exotic locales that were his natural habitat, in this case to an "unfrequented and distant Japanese isle" (87) in the far Pacific, where much of the action is played out.

It is an intensely moralistic tale, sentimentally told. Its central thesis is one that was to become very popular in the many subsequent Burroughs novels: the redemption of a "bad" man as the result of his falling in love with a "good" woman. Billy Byrne, the mucker, "was a product of the streets and alleys of Chicago's great West Side," where he fell in with the local gangs and distinguished himself for his great physical size and prowess. The novelistic underpinning for this narrative is that of the bildungsroman. The early pages of the book bristle with the language and imagery of education, [14] and this early Chicago schooling of Billy Byrne is subsequently continued by the aristocratic Barbara Harding when the two are shipwrecked and begin to fall in love.

Few Burroughs novels contain quite the dramatic metamorphosis of a central character that occurs in *The Mucker*. The series of coincidences that bring people and plot elements together is, once more, just short of outrageous, and the novel is thematically quintessential Burroughs. The curious race of "medieval" samurai living on the island where the second half of the tale takes place is simply another version of the strange civilization of Opar in the early Tarzan novels. The romantic interests are all paralleled in other early stories, most notably the Tarzan tales, and the regeneration or rebirth of Billy Byrne is mapped onto the standard Burroughs pattern of the *katabasis*. Thus the hero leaves the real world (America), faces "monsters" on the ship and on the island, rescues a friend and a woman, and finally returns to America, a man changed very much for the better as a result of his educational odyssey. As one critic has put it, the book "might stand as the archetype of the pulp adventure story . . . it provides glimpses of a full spectrum of settings and themes. In a single book it is virtually a catalog of the pulps."[15]

In late 1921 and early 1922 Burroughs wrote what must be considered his most naturalistic novel, *The Girl from Hollywood.*

Although it is far removed in tone and theme from the science-fiction series and the jungle adventures of Tarzan, there are certain points of contact, such as the wholesomeness of living in nature and the redemptive power of love.

The latter theme appears here as the reverse of its usual form, for in this tale it is a corrupted woman (rather than man) in love with a noble man (instead of woman) who is redeemed. The natural living involves no jungle, but the countryside, the rustic landscape as opposed to the defiling urban world. Indeed, at one point the author states explicitly the emblematic value of the Pennington ranch as antithesis to Hollywood: "a part of the pastoral allegory of content that was the Rancho del Ganado; and over all were the blue California sky and the glorious sun" (94). [16]

The plot is rather complicated, overlaid with contrasting subplots, but moves inexorably toward a denunciation of the concept "Hollywood." It is impossible here not to see a reflection of Burroughs's own bitter experience with the movie industry. Thus, *The Girl from Hollywood* turns into a morality play, exposing in a Zolaesque vein the corrupting influences of urban ambitions and the overarching greed for power and wealth.

Some thirteen years after Burroughs's death, a manuscript-length novel was discovered in the author's papers. Although this story, *Pirate's Blood,* is relatively short and has many marks of incompleteness about it, it is, conceptually, one of the more interesting narratives penned by Burroughs. A sign of this incompleteness is the lengthy and overworked description of the hero's journey across the Pacific. And the abrupt conclusion has the earmark of a hasty wrap-up that might well have been elaborated at the expense of the tedious report on the trip in the dirigible.

The plot stretches credulity to its limits: a descendant of the pirate Jean Lafitte grows up in a typical American town, goes to college, but is not quite bright enough to pass the bar exam. As a policeman, he ends up, after a series of admittedly bizarre circumstances, flying across the Pacific to somewhere in the South China Sea in a dirigiblelike contraption, where he lands among pirates. Here he joins first one gang, then another, and in the process falls in love with the mistress of the first and discovers that the mistress of the second is his old high-school sweetheart (who, having sunk so low, commits suicide). After a number of double-crosses and cutthroat battles, he leaves piracy, with the first pirate's ex-mistress, and settles down, apparently, to a comfortable life in Paris.

The interplay in the novel between the forces of heredity and environment has about it an indeterminate, groping character. It is surely suggestive that the novel, dealing with a woman's downfall through alcohol, was written *(but never published)* at precisely that period (the early 1930s) when Burroughs's first wife's drinking problems had gotten quite out of hand. It is tempting to suggest that the story is an effort on his part to try to come to some kind of understanding, no matter how inchoate, of what was happening to his wife, but that the closely personal nature of the underlying theme prevented him from offering the material for print.

It will of course never be known just what the truth in the matter is, but it must be granted that this late addition to the Burroughs canon raises interesting and unanswerable questions about the relationship of his personal life (as opposed to personal beliefs, which are everywhere evident in his works) to his literary activity.

Historical era. The two novels in the Apache series, *The War Chief* and *Apache Devil*, were written in 1926 and 1927 respectively. In them Burroughs looks at the "civilizing" of the American Southwest by the white man. The latter does not come off favorably. Long before it became chic to favor the Indian side of this part of American history, Burroughs took a decidedly pro-Indian stand in his depiction of the education and maturation of the Apache foundling, Shoz-Dijiji. Tarzan was a British lord saved from extinction at the hands of the ape Kerchak by the female anthropoid Kala; Andy MacDuff, infant son of Scottish Jerry MacDuff and his Cherokee wife, is saved from braining at the hands of the cruel chief Juh by the greater chief Go-yat-thlay, also know as Geronimo. Geronimo takes him back to camp and has his wife raise the foundling as his own.

Just as Tarzan in a sense became a better ape than the apes, Andy MacDuff proves to be a better Apache than the Apaches. And like Tarzan, who slew the great Bolgani the gorilla at the age of ten, Andy slays the great Black Bear, Shoz-Dijiji, in single combat at the age of ten, and takes his name from the victim. As Tarzan is different from his fellows, so is Shoz-Dijiji: he values education, in particular learning the language of his enemies (English), and he refuses to participate in the savage torture of captives or the mutilation of dead victims, in which many[17] of the Apaches indulge.

And like Tarzan, Shoz-Dijiji sufficiently distinguishes himself that he becomes heir apparent to leadership of the Apache federation.

The novel is in effect a brief for the Indian viewpoint. Since Shoz-Dijiji is half white and half Indian, he, like Tarzan, dwells in two worlds, both of which pull at him and function also as an emblem of reconciliation of opposing forces. Throughout the novel the mutual hatred of white (and Mexican) and Indian for each other is underscored, and yet there is a strong subtheme of the frowardness of such attitudes, arising from ingrained prejudice and lack of understanding on both sides. Burroughs's insistence on heredity over education and environment is pulled into play in this connection, for it is the un-Apache-like mindset of Shoz-Dijiji, deriving from his genetically mixed background, that enables him to begin to bridge the differences between Indian and white.

This theme of reconciliation of the two cultures is further underlined in the romantic interest that develops in the novel's second half between Wichita Billings and Shoz-Dijiji. After his Indian betrothed is killed through the carelessness of Juh (who is destroyed in a climactic battle with Shoz-Dijiji), his enforced contact with Wichita causes him to fall in love with her—and her with him. But on the final page of the story Shoz-Dijiji's declaration of love is rebuffed by Wichita, and the Indian rides off into the wilderness while she returns to her father's ranch. She realizes, of course, that she is in love with the Apache, but only too late. This sense of romantic disequilibrium at the end of the tale assures, as it did in the case of the first Tarzan novel, that a sequel is forthcoming. [18]

The book contains a powerful peroration stating the case of the Indian over against the alleged benevolence of the Bureau of Indian Affairs. The words of Shoz-Dijiji to Wichita Billings, who pleads with him to become a reservation Indian, anticipate later rhetoric on the subject of the American Indian. The passage is too long to cite, but the concluding exchange goes as follows:

"I am sorry," she said. "I never thought of it from your side. I can see that in some ways you are right; but in others you are wrong. All white men are not bad."

"All Indians are not bad," he replied quickly, "but the pindah-lickoyee [viz. "white-eyes"] treat them all alike—bad." (211)

The reader should not assume, however, that this story of the white-Indian Shoz-Dijiji is sheer moralizing. It is not. Indeed, it is, like the Tarzan and John Carter stories, a hero tale. It is, like so many of the other hero tales of Burroughs, cast in a recognizable format of heroic deeds, journeys to symbolic death-realms, and other patterns of myth. In order to win his bride, for example, Shoz-Dijiji must have fifty horses for her father, and he therefore sets off on a long journey into an uncompromising landscape in order to return with his herd and win his woman. This substory occupies some twenty pages, and, typically, Shoz-Dijiji is (mistakenly) believed by the other Indians to be dead, only to return miraculously later in the story. Burroughs himself has little hesitation in suggesting to the informed reader just how this story is to be viewed, for at its end he informs us as follows:

How he took them, alone and unaided, across those weary, burning miles, through scorching deserts and rugged mountains equally scorching, along a trail beset by enemies, pursued by wrathful vaqueros, would well have been the subject of a deathless epic had Shoz-Dijiji lived in the days of Homer. . . .
  Shoz-Dijiji had indeed performed a feat worthy of the greatest heroes of his race.
  Already he had crossed the boundary and was safe in the country of the Cho-kon-en. . . . (149)

Although *The War Chief* is at times overwritten, it is not a bad story. It is more overtly a message-tale than is usual for Burroughs, but perhaps his own personal involvement in the general locale and ambience of this story accounts for the more intensely personal[19] strain that seeps through the narrative.

Chapter Six
Concluding Assessment

An author of Burroughs's prodigious output (some seventy novels) and unflagging popularity might well be expected to have given rise to a huge secondary literature. Yet serious and sustained studies of the man and his writings are relatively few.[1] At the same time it must be noted that brief articles with a narrow focus on individual volumes or restricted aspects of Burroughs novels have appeared from time to time in both general and academic publications,[2] and partial surveys or brief comments can be found in some of the general studies on "pulp" literature and science fiction.[3]

Longer Studies

The ensuing section will concentrate on the book-length analyses of Burroughs and his novels done by five[4] writers: Henry Hardy Heins, Richard A. Lupoff, Michael Orth, Irwin Porges, and Erling B. Holtsmark, the present author.

Henry Hardy Heins. The first book-length work devoted to an aspect of Edgar Rice Burroughs's fiction is the monumental project entitled *A Golden Anniversary Bibliography of Edgar Rice Burroughs* by Henry Hardy Heins (West Kingston, R.I.: Donald M. Grant, 1962, 1964). Heins has worked out the publication history of Burroughs's works both as stories in magazines and as books, and further, offers a horde of useful and interesting information about Burroughs. The volume also contains some Burroughs items otherwise difficult to find.

Richard A. Lupoff. The distinction of undertaking the first sustained critical study of Edgar Rice Burroughs, however, goes to Richard A. Lupoff,[5] who subsequently published a specialized study given over to Burroughs's Martian cycle.[6]

The merits of Lupoff's two volumes are many, not the least of which is a genuine affection for Burroughs which, nonetheless, fails to blunt his critical acuity. Perhaps the most laudatory point about Lupoff's first book is his insistence that Burroughs be taken seriously, a point pursued with more focused enthusiasm in the special study of the Martian books.

In the former book he undertakes an organized survey of the entire corpus, and concludes with his own recommendations for a basic Burroughs library. This study is not so much a critical evaluation of Burroughs as it is a thorough analysis of the possible sources of his writings. Thus, in the case of the Tarzan material, for example, he discusses at length the literature on the feral child and humans who are alleged to have lived among animals. The lengthy work on this subject by Rudolph Altrochi[7] is given full consideration in this connection, as is the problematical relationship between Burroughs and Kipling and Burroughs and Haggard (chap. 15, "Ancestors of Tarzan," 215–30). Lupoff's book is of great value for the source-hunter, and in addition imparts a good sense of the vast range, in respect both to subject matter and quality, of Burroughs's varied writings. The tracing out of possible lines of descent from earlier and contemporary writers of science fiction like Jules Verne, H. G. Wells, Edwin Lester Arnold and others is quite thorough and balanced, and a good deal also appears about the naturalistic novels like *The Efficiency Expert* and *The Girl from Farris's*.

While Lupoff docs a masterly job of looking at the immediate ancestors of Burroughs's literary creations, he is almost totally silent about the ancient background—the heroic and mythic literature of antiquity. Incidental comments about Lucian (50) and even Homer (103) are never developed in any systematic way, and the reader certainly gains no sense of Burroughs's indebtedness to ancient writers for his own heroic cycles. Because Lupoff's book does contain so much detailed information, moreover, it is a serious flaw that it contains no index of any kind. This lack detracts from its great usefulness for the Burroughs researcher.

In his second book, dealing specifically with the Martian stories, Lupoff is much more the critic and less the searcher for literary sources. Several themes dominate his discussion: Mars was Burroughs's private enchanted forest, and the hero, John Carter, "a sort of dream-fantasy surrogate for Burroughs as he pursued his rise on another world" (134); "the books have several levels of meaning, some of them probably obscure to Burroughs himself" (18); and the complete series was "the adventure story of the developing human psyche" (21) and as "John Carter progresses from crawling infant to full manhood, so too does the personality of Edgar Rice

Burroughs, with the Martian books providing a window upon Burroughs' psyche through which the reader observes this process" (154). This latter is an interesting if traditional view, applicable to almost any author, which may nonetheless well be true of Burroughs. Lupoff likewise underscores the mythic dimension of the Martian books (8, 40, 89, 131, and 154 [cited below]):

There is a mythic verity to the stories, an aspect of utmost urgency and quite naive honesty, which gives the Martian cycle an appeal worlds beyond that of most stories of greater sophistication and control. These stories call out to the human psyche at a largely unconscious level, they call up the suppressed urges of the primitive man to take sword in hand and confront once and for all the vexatious world around him, they manipulate the most powerful of human archetypes.

It would certainly have been of critical value for Lupoff to have explored in more specific detail these mythic elements in Burroughs, since they are in fact so fundamental to all his fantasy fiction.

Although Lupoff is clearly a lover of Burroughs's fiction, he is also honest enough as critic to feel no compunction about pointing up some of the more egregious shortcomings of Burroughs's fiction. Thus, he rightly calls attention to the endless repetitiousness of the novels, going so far as to call *Synthetic Men of Mars* "one of the poorest of Burroughs' roughly seventy books" (68) and "a disastrous pastiche of Burroughs' own works larded over with countless cliches borrowed from the worst of the horror pulp fiction and the monster movies of the day" (50). And although he saw Burroughs as a "highly talented craftsman" (68), he also recognized that his manner of composing and creating Mars was "piecemeal . . . more of a patchwork than a mosaic pattern" (73); that Burroughs relied too much on "auctorial fiat" (83) and allowed "numerous inconsistencies and dangling ends that pervade the cycle" (24); and that the hero, John Carter, was "a rather one-dimensional adventure hero . . . physically attractive but in a bland, collar-ad sort of way" (14), while his wife, Dejah Thoris, is "inert" and "doesn't *do* anything" (36). After all, "serious characterization was [not] Burrough's great strength" (35).

On balance, Lupoff's two books are favorable toward Burroughs and, having the merit of being the first to develop a serious and sustained criticism of his works, will always remain part of the critical canon of the secondary Burroughs literature.

Irwin Porges. The publication of *Edgar Rice Burroughs: The Man Who Created Tarzan* in 1975 must be seen as a milestone in the history of Burroughs scholarship. Before that time no serious biography had appeared, and Porges's massive (819 large-format pages) study is likely to remain the standard reference for some time to come.

The book is an inordinately detailed accounting of Burroughs's life and works, beginning with his parents and earlier ancestors, and ending with his death in 1950. Although generally sympathetic to his subject, Porges adopts the healthy stance of objective analyst. He does a fine job of placing Burroughs in the milieu of the late-nineteenth century Midwest and, later, the hectic world of wealth and power in the Southern California of the twenties and thirties. Burroughs emerges in full clarity as child, youth, frustrated family man, and successful author; he is presented as the common, unpretentious individual that, by all accounts, he was, and his problems and weaknesses as human being are paraded next to the strengths and triumphs.

Porges also allocates considerable space to brief synopses of the novels, as well as a certain amount of criticism. The latter is understandably not emphasized, for the central focus of this study is the family into which Burroughs was born, the family that he himself started, and the often complex business dealings in which his career as writer of popular fiction involved him.

The real strength of Porges's biography for the literary critic of Burroughs is the masterful tracing of the latter's education and formative years. From specific courses in the curriculum at Phillips Academy in Andover, Massachusetts, for example, to the kind of reading that Burroughs enjoyed, Porges manages to impart a catholic understanding of what went into the shaping of the young Burroughs's attitudes and intellect. Such information is of immeasurable importance for any serious student of the relationship among the writer, his writings, and his world. For even if any author ought to be comprehensible merely in terms of his works, a biography like Porges's enables the critic to apply controls external to the text on suppositions and theories arising primarily, and properly, from the text itself.

In view, finally, of the indescribable wealth of factual information contained in this biography, it redounds to the book's credit that it is provided with a comprehensive index.

Michael Orth.   Orth's essays (see chap. 1, note 2) on Burroughs fall somewhere between straight source research and criticism, focusing on a kind of psycho-biographical analysis of the author. Orth sees Burroughs's writing as largely a matter of his attempt, first, to relieve the frustration of continued failure, and, second, to exorcise the demons of guilt and spiritual ennui allegedly created by his spectacular success in the market place. Much in Orth's speculation about Burroughs is of considerable interest, but is ultimately susceptible to neither proof nor disproof. The form of the presentation appears to follow a current fashion in contemporary biography, that of explaining the unhappy success.

It is surely true, as Orth points out, that Burroughs had a number of personal problems, including financial ones, but since these are the kinds of snarls that most men encounter in the mid-stages of their life, there is nothing unique about Burroughs in this respect. Nor does it seem plausible to suggest that his creative output can be explained within a reductive framework of personal anxieties sublimated, however many or complicated these all too human difficulties may have been.

In common with others, Orth thinks of Burroughs as a writer almost in spite of himself. There is a kind of romantic view of creativity that is invoked in the case of Burroughs, who, it seems, produced his numerous stories without really knowing what he was doing, almost as if by pure chance. This notion about Burroughs's apparently unwitting ability as a writer is not shared by the present author, nor does a critic like Lupoff appear to put much stock in it. Second thought should likewise be directed at Orth's various characterizations of Tarzan, who is said to be, among other things, inarticulate and somehow without relationship to language; surely a person who taught himself to read, was fascinated by words, and knew perhaps twenty languages (including Latin, classical Greek, Inca, Arabic, various African dialects, and major European languages) should hardly be so described.

Since Orth's work was done before Porges's biography appeared, it is possible that some of the views expressed at that time might now be subject to a certain amount of modification. To be singled out for commendation, however, is Orth's judicious treatment of the whole question of Burroughs's racism. As Orth shows, this attitude was part of the cultural baggage of Burroughs's age; yet, it is an uncomfortable area that anybody writing on Burroughs today must come to some kind of terms with. And Orth does an exemplary job, fair and to the point, neither castigating Burroughs from the arrogant vantage of hindsight nor exonerating him with slick platitudes. Orth's ferreting out of secondary literature is also highly commendable. Readers of his essays will gain a strong sense of what has been written about Burroughs both incidentally in mainline scholarly surveys of fantasy literature and also in the many so-called fanzines that have grown up as an important cottage industry around the Burroughs works.

Erling B. Holtsmark. Published in 1981, *Tarzan and Tradition: Classical Myth in Popular Literature* is the first book devoted exclusively to a study of the literary Tarzan. It offers a detailed analysis of the first six novels in the series, taking as its underlying theme that Burroughs wrote the tale of the apeman in the tradition of the heroic literature of classical antiquity. Burroughs was educated in Latin and classical Greek, and had by his own admission a lifelong interest in classical mythology and things ancient, especially Roman.

The first two chapters are given over to a rigorous discussion of Burroughs's use of language and rhetorical as well as narrative techniques. Classical in conception as well as execution, these are traced as a development from Burroughs's own study of Latin and Greek. Subsequent chapters take up in turn the deployment of the animals in Tarzan's jungle world, the unmistakably classical imprint of the hero himself, and the thematic concerns that are expressed throughout the works. Among these latter are Burroughs's strong interest in Darwinism, death and rebirth, and relationships within the family.

In the later chapters of the book an aggressive case is made for the generally mythical background to the series, not merely in the case of the hero, but also of the villains, heroines and, especially, the animals. A brief section on etymological analysis of many of the names that appear in the stories points likewise to the strong classical underpinning for the whole Tarzan mythos. An attempt is likewise made to indicate the Amerindian background in the makeup of the literary Tarzan, in particular the hero's characteristic sense of humor and tricksterism.

This work takes an extreme position in that it pushes to the limit interpretations *possible* from a very close reading of Burroughs's text, coupled with the facts now known from Porges's biography about Burroughs's education and reading habits. Where other critics have concentrated on the literary milieu of Burroughs's own day in their discussion of Tarzan, this book pushes the source back several thousand years. Some will no doubt be intrigued by its methodology and conclusions; others will find them far-fetched and quite unconvincing. As the first serious book-length study of the early Tarzan, however, this work will have to be confronted, whether pro or contra, by future researchers and critics of the Burroughs's phenomenon.

Briefer References

Other critics have also addressed themselves in varying degrees to aspects of Burroughs's fiction, both in more general works and in individual articles. A few suggestive examples are adduced below.

General works.   Incidental opinions and information about Burroughs and his writings, notably the scientific romances, will be found in many of the now numerous anthologies and studies of science fiction and fantasy literature. Regardless of the position that individual works adopt in their evaluation of Burroughs, they are all but unanimous about his high importance in the rise of popular American fiction. A mere sampling of the critical spectrum is possible.

Even during Burroughs's lifetime, his works came up for serious discussion. Among the earliest are the comments of J. O. Bailey in his *Pilgrims Through Space and Time: Trends and Patterns in Scientific and Utopian Fiction* (New York: Argus Books, 1947). Although Bailey is surely correct in seeing Tarzan as a myth-figure, he is less than impressed with the works. In discussing the thirteenth Tarzan novel, *Tarzan at the Earth's Core,* he suggests, without much supporting commentary, that the "book, like all the Tarzan books, is all excitement, hair-breadth escapes, scraps of evolutionary theory, slices of scrambled geology and paleontology, and fragments taken from the traditions of scientific fiction" (317). Nor is Kingsley Amis, in his *New Maps of Hell: A Survey of Science Fiction* (New York: Harcourt, Brace & Co., 1960) a great fan of what he terms Burroughs's "dreadfully fluent pen," but gives very little accounting for this opinion. At the same time, Amis is willing to admit that Tarzan is "a more complicated person than the continuing spate of films about him would suggest" (45), a point that must be seconded with cheers.

The well-known critic of science fiction, Sam Moskowitz, takes a different tack. In his *Explorers of the Infinite: Shapers of Science Fiction* (New York: World Publishing Co., 1963), he calls Burroughs "a natural storyteller" with "an unsurpassed sense of pace" (175), and offers the suggestion that Tarzan "elevated him to literary greatness" (176), for the apeman is "one of the world's great romances" (177). In commenting on Burroughs's science fiction, Moskowitz asserts that it "is a direct descendant of the travel tale typified by the *Odyssey*" (174), and one wishes that he had explored this proposition in more detail. The Venus series is, according to Moskowitz, "not among his better works" (187), a view shared by many critics, including the present one. A later book by Moskowitz, an anthology with commentary, *Under the Moons of Mars: A History and Anthology of "The Scientific Romance" in the Munsey Magazines, 1912–1920* (New York: Holt, Rinehart & Winston, 1970) similarly takes a positive view of Burroughs's creations. Moskowitz here asserts that the publication of the first Martian tale in 1912 "turned the entire direction of science fiction from prophecy and sociology to romantic adventure . . . and became *the* major influence on the field through 1934" (291). Although Moskowitz recognizes problematical aspects to Burroughs (e.g., the possibility of "borderline racism in his handling of African savages" [298], he is perhaps the most enthusiastic of early mainline critics in his advocacy of Burroughs's fiction.

The same cannot be said for Ron Goulart's snide commentary in *Cheap Thrills: An Informal History of the Pulp Magazines* (New Rochelle: Arlington House, 1972). Adopting an Olympian posture of supercilious disdain, he pillories Burroughs with one clever turn of phrase after another. Regrettably, such serious criticism of Burroughs as lurks beneath the shimmering surface of Goulart's self-satisfied prose never emerges in any effective clarity.

The lengthy *Billion Year Spree: The True History of Science Fiction* (Garden City: Doubleday & Company, 1973) by Brian W. Aldiss takes a somewhat ambivalent stance. Aldiss, however, is not out to make points from his critical targets, and puts forth thoughtful comments about Burroughs's fiction. Although he appreciates the narrative élan, he is not impressed with Burroughs as crafter of words. As to what Burroughs may have been up to, Aldiss suggests that he was "teaching us not to think. Of course, Burroughs is teaching us to wonder" (158). Aldiss has an interesting comparison of Burroughs's *Pellucidar* with H. G. Wells's *Men Like Gods,* in which he addresses the differing modes of fantasy as opposed to analysis, respectively, in the two authors (156–58, 168). Aldiss is scrupulously fair in his critique of Burroughs, and appears unwilling either to condemn or praise outright.

Articles. Not many papers have appeared on Burroughs in academic journals devoted to literary and cultural criticism. A fair amount has found its way into the popular press over the years, most of it taking a quite negative attitude. A representative survey of both reviews of new books and critical appraisals of various aspects of Burroughs's writings will be found in the introduction to the author's *Tarzan and Tradition: Classical Myth in Popular Literature* (3–6).

Academic critics have, however, not maintained absolute silence on this subject in the journals, and two are here singled out. In a favorable paper on Burroughs's two Apache novels,[8] Robert E. Morsberger gives reasoned praise to Burroughs's version of the Apache Wars at the end of the last century. He lauds their realism and historical accuracy, and quite rightly points out that they took a favorable and sympathetic view of the Indians long before that attitude came into popular fashion. He characterizes the books as "intensely serious and meticulously accurate" (280), and comments on their irony, eloquence, and stylistic merit ("stylistically, his dialogue and descriptions are far better than Fenimore Cooper's, and modern readers conditioned to scoff at Burroughs may forget that he was first praised for his style" [283]). The hero of the set, Shoz-Dijiji, is seen as a fairly complex literary personality, both as individual and symbol. Morsberger offers a sensitive analysis of the amatory interest in the books, and discusses the important thematic development of a cultural pull in the two conflicting directions of civilization and savagery. Indeed, a basic point that Burroughs makes in the Apache series is that "civilization" is not necessarily more just or better than the Indian way, nor, again, necessarily worse. As Morsberger points out, "Burroughs avoids the pitfall of ennobling all one race and vilifying another. His Apaches are neither the devils of the movie *Geronimo* nor the saints of the movie *Broken Arrow*" (286).

In a somewhat different vein, Gary Topping addresses some of the underlying thematic concerns of the Tarzan series.[9] Comparing Burroughs with Zane Grey, he gets at the conflicting impulses of these authors' heroes that push them alternately in the directions of escape and isolation from civilization on the one hand, and the attempt to embrace it, on the other. Topping uses the term "pastoral" as metaphor for the successful mediation of these two disparate trends, categorizing both authors as prominent popular representatives of the so-called "wilderness cult" of the years 1890–1920 in American society. Tarzan's problem is seen as his inability to fit, finally, into either the world of the apes in the jungle or that of men in the cities of civilization. The closest that Tarzan comes, on this view, to finding a personal solution to his crisis of identity is the Bedouin world that he briefly encounters in *The Return of Tarzan* ("he finds in their society a pastoral equilibrium between the extremes of the city and the jungle" [15]). Topping's final assessment of the two authors is very much to the point:

> Grey, then, succeeded somewhat better than Burroughs in creating a pastoral metaphor that would point toward a means of retaining the best of the frontier's contribution to American culture. . . . None of Grey's characters is as interesting as Tarzan; Grey thus was not tempted to abandon his cultural purpose to exploit their psychology. Burroughs may be of more interest to the literary critic (he shows in many ways a greater skill as a writer than Grey), but Grey is of more interest to the cultural historian. (22)

Final Critique of Burroughs

The position of Edgar Rice Burroughs as a giant among popular writers of the twentieth century is secure beyond doubt. Evaluation of his works is more problematical, however, ranging from contemptuous dismissal to hyperbolic and uncritical acceptance.

Stylistically, Burroughs was more than a competent writer, if not consistent. He was clearly capable of a high style of considerable psychological depth, but was either unwilling or incapable of sustaining such an effort throughout any single volume. And there is ample evidence in the corpus of the great speed with which he composed, from grammatical errors to the larger infelicities of awkward sentence structure and uncontrolled lexical baroqueness.

As crafter of narrative, Burroughs was, as has been said by more than one critic, a natural storyteller. He was gifted with a quite remarkable sense of pace and ability to juggle two or even three subordinate and parallel narratives. Here, too, however, he had a tendency to let plot get ahead of planning. Hence the profusion of shameless coincidences that came increasingly to be required in order to make stories "come out" in the end. Endings, or resolutions, are often quite abrupt and weakly motivated, betraying a lack of careful thinking about the meshing of plot elements. At the same time, Burroughs was a master at creating, within the story itself, genuine excitement and interest in what is to happen next: few writers of any kind have been able to generate the sheer narrative rush which Burroughs seemed quite naturally to have been able to develop.

A more serious criticism of Burroughs as writer attaches to this last point. Because he was so enamored of merely telling a tale—which few deny that he did with masterful competence—he all too often let opportunities for a deepening of his literary creations slip out of his grasp. Situations set up are not followed through, and expectations arising out of the profoundly traditional and mythic cast of his works are never met. Above all, a reader in touch with literary tradition is frequently disappointed that this or that line of enquiry, almost teasingly started, is never fully developed. Gary Topping, in discussing Burroughs's failure to follow through in certain ways in his characterization of Tarzan, makes a comment that merits repeating for its general validity in respect to a central weakness in Burroughs's output:

Burroughs . . . became trapped in a literary tautology in developing the character of Tarzan: Tarzan is a savage who is unhappy in civilization, yet he is a civilized man who is unhappy in the jungle. Burroughs became so fascinated by the pathos of that situation that he allowed it to drive him past the opportunities that arose for breaking the cycle. The fact that he did so is unfortunate, for he thereby missed a chance to deepen an already fascinating story by adding to it an element of cultural significance that it presently lacks. (22)

One might rephrase the thinking behind this last observation. It is not so much a question of any lack of "cultural significance" as of failure by Burroughs to follow through in a more serious and sustained fashion than he does on the personal and societal implications already present in the tangible difficulties of his heroes and heroines. Thus, solutions are generally speaking always limited to the physical extrication from danger, and very little, especially in the later books, is done with the question of existential or ontological resolutions to problems faced by individuals and societies.

It might be argued that such criticism is unfair, for Burroughs never meant to dig into "deep" ground. The fact remains that, despite his own claims not to have intended anything beyond mere entertainment in his stories, he did broach a large number of issues that have been and continue to be of central importance in Western culture: the value of the individual in relation to the state; the significance of man's cultural and social capacities over and against his more primitive passions; the negatives and positives of "progress" in science and technology; man's relationship to his natural environment; the proper role of religion in public and private life; the respective roles of men and women in their associations with each other; and (to cut a long list short) man's treatment of his fellow man, however different in appearance and outlook. These and other issues are persistently hinted at and raised in Burroughs's novels, even the worst of them, and it is therefore regrettable that so little serious engagement in the *issues* is encountered. To be sure, *Tarzan the Terrible* (a quite good novel), for example, raises by strong implication the question of racial prejudice, as does *Land of Terror* (perhaps Burroughs's most mindless novel), but neither does much more than that, more than merely raising the question. Awareness, yes, but the spinning out of possible solutions, rarely. By contrast, in a book like *Jungle Tales of Tarzan*, it is clear that Burroughs is capable of engaging in a reasonably elaborate analysis of a central problem in Western philosophy: the distinction between reality and appearance. True, no philosopher is likely to be satisfied with Burroughs's discussion or answer, but the point is that a serious issue is not only raised but taken seriously and allotted some thought. Thus, again as with his stylistic competence as opposed to performance, it is not that Burroughs was unable to deal at a deeper level with issues that he raised, but, apparently, simply was not much interested in doing so. One wishes, finally, that Burroughs had not been so profligate in wasting available opportunities.

That, however, is the kind of writer he was. Although it is hard to imagine that, now going on four generations of avid readers, Burroughs will ever disappear from the landscape of American literature, he will never be counted among the greats. Although his works deal at one level with many of the same issues that appear in mainline serious fiction from the time of Homer to the present, it is their lack of a consistent confrontation with the deeper implications of their own concerns that will keep them forever in the ranks of the "popular." With few exceptions (e.g., the early Tarzan novels), there is little notion in Burroughs of the genuine complexity of human existence and the intractable difficulty of sorting out and evaluating a multiplicity of behavioral alternatives for survival in civilized societies. To suggest, for example, as Burroughs repeatedly does, that civilization is corrupt and hypocritical is simply not enough, no matter how true the suggestion may be. For the implied solution—being transported to Mars or growing up a hero in the jungle—has no bearing on the living of real lives in a real world.

In conclusion, it is precisely this devotion to fantasy and the possibilities envisioned by a fruitful imagination untrammeled with strictures of realism that have offended so many critics of Burroughs. Yet, herein lies the eternally endearing quality of the man's works as escapist fiction. While it does not compel us to think much or in overly serious ways about ourselves and our lives, it shares in the shaping of our dreams. And that is not bad for a fellow who set out to do a little entertaining and at the same time support his family.

Thank God, I say, for Edgar Rice Burroughs.

Notes and References

Chapter One

1. One critic has gone to great lengths to point out what he deems to be the hero's very American and undesirable trait of imposing his will and ways on a foreign culture. See John T. Flautz, "An American Demagogue in Barsoom," *Journal of Popular Culture* 1 (1967) 263–75.

2. Throughout this book, and in particular in this introductory chapter on Burroughs's biographical background, I make reference to the monumental biography of the author written by Irwin Porges, *Edgar Rice Burroughs: The Man Who Created Tarzan* (Provo, 1975). I am eager to acknowledge an inestimable debt to Porges's meticulous detailing of the facts of Burroughs's long and interesting life, and echo the observation made in that book's foreword by Burroughs's son Hulbert: "This book will be a prime, standard source for all future Burroughs researchers."

Anyone wishing to know more about the life and times of Burroughs than can possibly be covered in the present brief chapter simply must consult Porges's book, which has appeared in paperback. Page references to Porges's work will be cited in the text with the abbreviation *ERB*.

Two other books merit mention in this connection, the first of which is a somewhat superficial account of Burroughs's life and works, the latter of which is an ingenious and humorous "biography" of Tarzan: Robert J. Fenton, *The Big Swingers* (Englewood Cliffs, 1967), and Philip Jose Farmer, *Tarzan Alive* (Garden City, 1972).

A series of articles in the fanzine *ERB-dom* (volumes 81–86 [1975–76]) by Michael Orth also merits serious attention. The articles are slanted toward a kind of psycho-biography of Burroughs, and contain many interesting observations about Burroughs and his output.

3. Besides the four who lived to grow up, two were stillborn and two died at an early age. Porges quotes a poignant recollection by Ed: "The earliest event in my life that I can recall clearly is the sudden death of an infant brother in my mother's arms" (*ERB*, 774).

4. *The Mucker, The Mad King, The Eternal Lover* (= "Nu of the Eocene"), *The Beasts of Tarzan, The Lad and the Lion, The Girl from Farris's*, and *Thuvia, Maid of Mars* (no. 4 in the Martian series).

Chapter Two

1. See in particular the article by Richard D. Mullen, "Edgar Rice Burroughs and the Fate Worse Than Death," *Riverside Quarterly* 4 (June 1970): 187ff.

2. Most notable here are the computerized missiles invented by Phor Tak in *A Fighting Man of Mars* (131f.) and the on-board computer built by Fal Sivas for his Jupiter-bound spacecraft in *Swords of Mars*.

3. Thus, in that prototypical Martian hell, the Valley Dor in *The Gods of Mars* (especially pages 28–52), it cannot be fortuitous that John Carter, taking note of the individuals he sees in that underworld, has the following to say:

> As they lay sprawled about the floor, sometimes overlapping one another, again in heaps of several bodies, they suggested instantly to me the grotesque illustrations that I had seen in copies of Dante's *Inferno*, and what more fitting comparison? Was this not indeed a veritable hell, peopled by lost souls, dead and damned beyond all hope? (54)

This is only the most obvious of many indications in the design of his narrative that Burroughs was articulating a well-defined strategy of mapping the traditional heroic journey to hell in the life cycle of his own hero.

4. Richard Lupoff, *Barsoom: Edgar Rice Burroughs and the Martian Vision,* (Baltimore, 1976), 17, has suggested that the mechanics of this initial transport of John Carter to Mars involved a drug-induced fantasy:

> Rather, the cave sequence, and probably the whole of *A Princess of Mars*—if not the whole Martian cycle—was intended on one level at least as a drugged fantasy induced by that "greenish powder." . . . in this period cannabis was quite legal and readily available. Both the physical description of the greenish powder and the "slight vapor" with its "slightly pungent odor" are suggestive of the latter herb.

5. This point is repeatedly made by Lupoff, *Barsoom,* 25, 27, 62, 63 ("Barsoom was Burroughs' psychic home"), 90, 92, 134, 135, 150 ("It is long since obvious that he [viz. John Carter] *is* Edgar Rice Burroughs.").

6. All traditional epic heroes embody the two personalities of lover and warrior. Indeed, the point had become a cliché already in antiquity, as is clear from the satirizing of the so-called *miles amator,* or "soldier-lover," of Plautine comedy, and was of course worked to death in the medieval and Renaissance portraits of the courtly lover who was also a militant crusader against the heathens.

7. Lupoff, *Barsoom,* 36, suggests, with some justification, that "John Carter is little more than a type," and on page 14 says that the warlord of Mars is "himself not, on the face of it, a very interesting character."

8. Chapter 8 ("The Spider of Ghasta") of *A Fighting Man of Mars* (103–116) is surely the most gruesome episode in the entire Martian series. It is unparalleled in sadistic intensity, and well conveys the sense of descent

into hell; in this chilling *katabasis* the grim god of death as host welcoming his unfortunate guests and the tortures of his victims are not without their mythic overtones: not only Odysseus and Aeneas view similar episodes, but also Dante, who likewise saw the tortures of wretched victims in the underworld.

9. The name (as often in Burroughs) is not without its compressed significance: the word means "sickness" in Latin. And as is clear from later events (in both this novel and the subsequent *Synthetic Men of Mars*), sickness is as trenchant and compendious a designation for this city of surgical apocalypse and teratological nightmare as one could want.

10. On page 34 of *Synthetic Men of Mars* John Carter is berating Ras Thavas for his folly in developing the vats of life, now (like the porridge-producing bowl of the fairy tale) unstoppable in their outpouring of protoplasm, and observes to him that he has "created a Frankensteinian host that will not only destroy you but the civilization of a world."

11. The name "Mors" is of course the standard Latin word for "death," from which all our related words on the stem "mort-" are derived.

12. A notable exception is the misfortune that befell Phao of Jahar, a slave in the court of the tyrant Haj Osis of Tjanath. She was quite clearly raped by the evil prison guard Yo Seno. Burroughs does not go into any detail, but an unmistakable allusiveness hovers about the girl's comment: "When I was a prisoner in that room, Yo Seno came thus to visit me. He is a beast" (*A Fighting Man of Mars*, 81). And the reaction of the hero Hadron, to whom she makes this statement, is sufficiently explicit to leave no doubt of what had happened to Phao.

13. Other heroines who would also lend themselves well to the discussion at hand are Tara of Helium (daughter of John Carter and Dejah Thoris) Llana of Gathol (daughter of Tara and Gahan of Gathol), Tavia of Jahar (who married the hero Tan Hadron of Hastor), Valla Dia of Duhor (who married Vad Varo [a.k.a. Ulysses Paxton of Virginia]), and many others less substantially delineated.

Chapter Three

1. Although some books (the most notable examples are Richard A. Lupoff, *Edgar Rice Burroughs: Master of Adventure*, rev. ed. [New York, 1968] and Porges, *Edgar Rice Burroughs*, do discuss the various creations of Burroughs in brief, the only full-length study of Tarzan in English appeared as recently as 1981 (Erling B. Holtsmark, *Tarzan and Tradition: Classical Myth in Popular Literature* [Westport, 1981]). The general nature of the present book makes it impossible to discuss the literary Tarzan in anything like the detail found in that volume. The work in French by Francis Lacassin (*Tarzan, ou le Chevalier Crispé* [Paris, 1971]) should be noted here; it deals more with Tarzan as he is represented in such media

as film and comic strips, but there is also some discussion of Tarzan the literary figure.

2. See N. Owen Rush, *The Diversions of a Westerner: With Emphasis upon Owen Wister and Frederic Remington* (Amarillo, 1979), 85.

3. In general, on this point of the classical debt see Holtsmark, *Tarzan and Tradition,* 30–32, 89–90, and passim.

4. Lupoff, *Edgar Rice Burroughs,* 227. Lupoff's chapter 15 ("Ancestors of Tarzan"), though somewhat idiosyncratic at times, is a masterful exposition of the modern antecedents. A strange silence reigns in regard to the ancient material, except for reference to Romulus and Remus.

5. The passage in question is line 4 of book 1 of Vergil's *Aeneid: "memorem Iunonis ob iram."*

6. On page 7 of the novel his father describes him to Tarzan: "[he] has spent the greater part of his time in pursuing his studies in various European universities, where he has specialized *in archaeology and the study of dead languages"* (my italics).

7. The name is itself evocative of one of the great quests of classical mythology, that of Jason and his Argonauts, best known to us today from the epic *Argonautica* by Apollonius of Rhodes (third century B.C.).

8. For a generalization about their influence on the Tarzan stories, see Holtsmark, *Tarzan and Tradition,* 131.

9. See, for example, page 131 of Porges, *Edgar Rice Burroughs:* "My research was for data concerning the fauna and flora of Africa and the customs of native tribes. . . . I had already found Tarzan in my own imagination."

10. See Porges, *Edgar Rice Burroughs,* 130. Cf. also 72, 129f., 132, 194, 544, and 606.

11. Holtsmark, *Tarzan and Tradition,* 49, 53. Consider also the following passages scattered throughout the corpus: *Tarzan and the Antmen* (37, 49, 98); *Tarzan at the Earth's Core* (71, 97); *Tarzan the Invincible* (71); *Tarzan Triumphant* (128f.); *Tarzan and the City of Gold* (27, 56); *Tarzan and the Leopard Men* (31, 55); *Tarzan and the Foreign Legion* (65); *Tarzan and the Madman* (144).

12. For a negative view of Burroughs's handling of the awakening sense of religiosity within the youthful Tarzan, see Brian V. Street, *The Savage in Literature: Representations of "Primitive" Society in English Fiction 1858–1920* (London, 1975), 170–75.

13. In portraying the petty and narrow interpretation that Angustus's descendants have given to religion, Burroughs no doubt intentionally selected this significant name. For the adjective *angustus* means "petty, narrow" in Latin, a language, along with classical Greek, that Burroughs knew and often drew on for his onomastic excursions. (See the thorough-going discussion of this matter in Holtsmark, *Tarzan and Tradition,* 87–

90 and 177 [note 10]). The patriarch of the line, then, is introduced to us, not unaptly, as "the narrow one."

14. A typical narrative ploy in the Tarzan novels is, as here, the existence of two antithetical civilizations or societies, in the sustained contrast between which the author comments, often in a serious if humorous and satirical vein, on issues relevant to his own day. Thus in the present case, the two societies of North and South Midian become vehicles for what is the most thorough-going critique in all the Tarzan novels of the absurd extremes to which religious impulse can carry men. Some other examples of this device are the opposing societies of Trohanadalmakus and Veltopismakus in the world of the Minunians (*Tarzan and the Antmen*, published in 1924), where the issues are public taxation and the differing postures on military preparedness; in *Tarzan, Lord of the Jungle*, where the Knights of Nimmr and the Knights of Sepulcher war with each other over a long-standing dispute as to whether the Holy Land still needs to be liberated or a return to England should be undertaken (98–99); in *Tarzan and the Lost Empire*, where bitter rivalry exists between the realms of Validus Augustus, ruler of Castrum Mare, and Sublatus, ruler of Castrum Sanguinarius, over the direct issue of economic and social organization; in *Tarzan and the City of Gold*, where the two civilizations of Athne, the city of ivory, and Cathne, the city of gold, are locked in combat over women and wealth. Burroughs's point of view about the silliness of this kind of sustained hostility is underlined by the fact that many of these warring societies make annual truces for the exchange of goods and participation in festivals.

15. See the study of Leo J. Henkin, *Darwinism in the English Novel 1860–1910: The Impact of Evolution on Victorian Fiction* (New York, 1940).

16. Blacks are generically represented as inferior to whites, although individual exceptions certainly occur (e.g., Mugambi in *Tarzan and the Jewels of Opar*); regrettably, the same can be said for a host of other nationalities (e.g., Arabs, Chinese, Germans, Japanese, Swedes), all of whom (with the exception of the propaganda-created Japanese of *Tarzan and the Foreign Legion* [written in 1944]) however, like the blacks, also have "good" representatives.

17. On this point, see Street, *Savage in Literature*, 77.

18. See *The Gods of Mars*, 68.

19. One critic is sufficiently impressed with *Tarzan and the Antmen* to call it the "high point in the Tarzan series and for that matter in Burroughs' entire career." See Lupoff, *Edgar Rice Burroughs*, 241.

20. The passage may well be modeled on that in book 5 of Vergil's *Aeneid* (lines 548–603), where the young Trojans put on an honorific display of skillful horsemanship. Here, too, the participants are *playing* at war.

Chapter Four

1. A likely candidate as exception to this observation might be *Tarzan and the Lion Man* with its bizarre concoction of humanoid apes who speak a version of Elizabethan English and the apelike scientist who has set himself up as their god.

2. It should be noted in this comparison between archers Odysseus and Tarzan that one of the defining emblems identifying Odysseus the beggar as Odysseus the master of Ithaca was his ability to bend the bow that no other person could bend. So, too, in *Tarzan and the City of Gold* is the bow of Tarzan characterized:

> Short but powerful was the bow of the ape- man; short, that it might be easily carried through the forest and the jungle; powerful, that it might send its shafts through the toughest hide to a vital organ of its prey. Such a bow was this that no ordinary man might bend it. (11)

3. Indeed, some of the comic artists who have done Tarzan have been not only great illustrators but quite interesting storytellers as well. One thinks in this connection in particular of Burne Hogarth's dynamically engaged Tarzan, and to some extent of the pre-Hogarth version of Hal Foster (who later developed Prince Valiant) and the post-Hogarth strips of Russ Manning. The subject of Tarzan's iconography is itself easily the subject for a separate book-length study, and would make a fascinating contribution to the study of both popular narrative and twentieth-century illustration.

4. Other examples are Ludon *(Tarzan the Terrible)*, Ibn-Jad and Bohun *(Tarzan, Lord of the Jungle)*, Kraski *(Tarzan and the Golden Lion)*, Validus Augustus and Fastus Sublatus *(Tarzan and the Lost Empire)*, Skruk and the Horibs *(Tarzan at the Earth's Core)*, the Oparians *(The Return of Tarzan* and *Tarzan and the Jewels of Opar)*, Abu-Bath and To-Yat *(Tarzan the Invincible)*, Mohammed Beyd and Taglat *(Tarzan and the Jewels of Opar)*, Terkoz *(Tarzan of the Apes)*, Stabutch *(Tarzan Triumphant)*, Erot *(Tarzan and the City of Gold)*, M'Duze and Xerstle *(Tarzan and the City of Gold)*, Lupingu *(Tarzan and the Leopard Men)*, Kavandavanda *(Tarzan's Quest)*, and Kumajiro Tada and Oju *(Tarzan and the Foreign Legion)*.

5. In the jungle society of Burroughs's world the great apes, among whom Tarzan lives, are a very different species from the gorillas, who are their mortal enemies.

6. Just such a passage (Tarzan's slaying of a lion and his accompanying victory cry) is analyzed in detail in Holtsmark, *Tarzan and Tradition*, 161–66.

7. See Robert J. Fenton, *The Big Swingers* (Englewood Cliffs, 1967), 11. Further, (psycho-)biographical readings of Burroughs's works may be

found in the articles by Michael Orth in the fanzine *ERB-dom* 81–86 (1975–76).

8. Family relationships in general occupy an important niche in the novels. Burroughs seems to have been quite intrigued with describing the many possible paths along which such associations can develop. In any event, numerous variations are spun on the basic configurations involving mother and son, father and son, and father and daughter (curiously, those involving mother and daughter are notable only for their almost total absence).

9. The pattern repeats itself. Not only is Jane subjected to a similar abduction by the ape Taglat in *Tarzan and the Jewels of Opar* (101f.), but Corrie van der Meer in *Tarzan and the Foreign Legion* is likewise carried off by the lusting orangutan Oju (118f.).

10. Frank Luther Mott, *Golden Multitudes: The Story of Best Sellers in the United States* (New York, 1947), 313.

11. Q. D. Leavis, *Fiction and the Reading Public* (London, 1932 [1965]), 40.

12. Mott, *Golden Multitudes,* 240.

13. This observation is recorded also by James D. Hart in *The Popular Book: A History of America's Literary Taste* (Berkeley, 1950, 1963), 220: "It is estimated . . . that about 25,000,000 copies of Tarzan of the Apes and its more than thirty [*sic*] sequels have been printed and sold in fifty-six languages."

14. Paul Mandel, "Tarzan of the Paperbacks," *Life* 55, no. 22 (29 November 1963), 11, asserts that between 1914 and 1940 all of Burroughs's "books sold 35 million copies."

15. Alice Payne Hackett, *70 Years of Best Sellers 1895–1965* (New York, 1967), 39.

16. Irving Harlow Hart, "The Most Popular Authors of Fiction in the Post-War Period, 1919–1926," *Publishers' Weekly* 111 (12 March 1927), 1046.

17. Irving Harlow Hart, "The One Hundred Leading Authors of Best Sellers in Fiction from 1895 to 1944," *Publishers' Weekly* 149 (19 January 1946), 288.

18. Mandel, "Tarzan of the Paperbacks," 12.

19. It is not entirely clear just why this happened, but it is surely in part due to expiration of copyrights, which put some of the works in the public domain. Fenton, *The Big Swingers,* pages 2f., and 4f., here following Mandel "Tarzan of the Paperbacks," page 11, has a further suggestion in the matter: a misinformed high-school librarian from Downey, California, in 1961 banned *Tarzan of the Apes* from the shelves on the (erroneous) grounds that Tarzan and Jane had had a son out of wedlock, thus making the whole story immoral. The media picked up this story

and generated an enormous interest in the works of Burroughs. The revival had begun.

20. Cf. Mandel "Tarzan of the Paperbacks," 11.

21. E. F. Bleiler, *Eight Dime Novels,* (New York, 1974), vii.

22. Ibid., ix. "The history of the dime novel, on the whole, is devolution."

23. See Tony Goodstone, *The Pulps: Fifty Years of American Pop Culture* (New York, 1970), v.

24. A lively account of what it was like to be a pulp writer in the twenties and later is found in Frank Gruber's *The Pulp Jungle* (Los Angeles, 1967). Gruber also mentions many of the "names" of the period.

25. In general, see the discursive work by Dorothy B. Hughes, *Erle Stanley Gardner: The Case of the Real Perry Mason* (New York, 1978).

26. Darrell C. Richardson, *Max Brand: The Man and his Work* (Los Angeles, 1952), comments that "Faust basically wrote fairy tales—but grown-up fairy tales" (105). In a similar and much more thorough vein, Robert Easton, *Max Brand: The Big "Westerner,"* (Norman, 1970), dwells at length on Brand's thoroughly mythical orientation to his writing (9, 21, 32f., 149–51, etc.). Like Burroughs, Brand had read (but in English translation only) widely in classical Greek and Latin literature, including the mythology. One is tempted to see this similarly mythic cast to their writings as at least partially responsible for the phenomenal and enduring popularity of each writer.

Chapter Five

1. Others that should be noted are those dealing with Caspak *(The Land that Time Forgot, The People that Time Forgot, and Out of Time's Abyss),* Poloda *(Beyond the Farthest Star and Tangor Returns),* the Apache Southwest *(The War Chief and Apache Devil),* and the lunar interior *(The Moon Maid, The Moon Men, and The Red Hawk* [in the latter two the action has moved to earth]).

2. The literary antecedents in English literature are traced in Lupoff, *Edgar Rice Burroughs,* 66–70. The descent into the bowels of earth, or the nether world, is of course preeminently a *katabatic* (see index under *ka-tabasis*) motif, and these novels are extended versions of this common Burroughs theme.

3. Although acutely aware of the shortcomings of his own world, Innes nonetheless believes that "it will not be long before Pellucidar will become as nearly a Utopia as one may expect to find this side of heaven" (190).

4. Lifting a page from the administrative manuals of the European colonizers of Africa, for example, Innes creates his federation by marking

"out as best we could natural boundaries dividing the various kingdoms. We had warned tribes beyond these boundaries that they must not trespass, and we had marched against and severely punished those who had" (45).

5. Note the preoccupation of Innes throughout the novel with the cartography of Pellucidar, an emblematic "mapping" of its status, which will enable him the better to chart its course for the future.

6. *Tarzan at the Earth's Core* was done in late 1928 and early 1929, immediately after the completion of *Tanar of Pellucidar* (finished in late November of 1928). In *Tarzan at the Earth's Core,* Jason Gridley, aptly named after the great classical hero who led the Argonauts to the unknown world beyond the Black Sea, occupies virtually equal billing with Tarzan as protagonist. The rescue that Gridley foretold at the end of *Tanar of Pellucidar* is effected, and Gridley in the bargain falls in love with the beautiful Jana of Zoram and decides to stay at the earth's core in Sari when Tarzan and the other members of the expedition return to the outside world.

7. The name is, again, at least in part significant. The first element (Am-) is the Latin stem for "love," and the last part (-cap) is the Latin stem for "take."

8. Lupoff, *Edgar Rice Burroughs,* 164.

9. Brian W. Aldiss, *Billion Year Spree: The True History of Science Fiction* (New York, 1973), 165.

10. The extreme linearity of these novels give them only the faintest hint of plot; as in the Pellucidar series, the emphasis is almost exclusively on sheer action, one event following breathlessly on another. As Lupoff has put it in *Edgar Rice Burroughs:* "The basic structure, if the term is even applicable, is extremely simple. Carson and Duare wander about the largely unknown lands and seas of Amtor, visiting various strange city-states. Most of the time they are either hiding or in flight" (161).

11. But in *Tarzan of the Apes,* for example, it is profitably employed in the formulaic sequence of Jane's involvement with Terkoz, Canler, Clayton, and Tarzan. See Holtsmark, *Tarzan and Tradition,* 143f. and appendix 1.

12. There are some dozen passages of this type in the Venus novels. Cf. *Pirates of Venus,* 40–46 (targo and "hyena"), 92–93 (targo), 96–98 (targo), and 105–8 (basto); *Lost on Venus,* 24–28 (snakes), 28–32 (tharban), 65–68 (basto), 68–71 (basto and tharban), 77–80 (vere), and 90–92 (kazars); and *Escape on Venus,* 46–47 (guypals), 182–86 (tharban and tongzan), and 264–65 (tharban).

13. The passages that might be referenced are numerous: for example, the cave at the start of *A Princess of Mars* when John Carter begins his

great journey; the shipwreck sequence in the middle of *The Return of Tarzan;* Tarzan's loss of memory in the treasure vaults of Opar in *Tarzan and the Jewels of Opar;* and so forth.

14. For example, "His kindergarten education had commenced in an alley. . . . (6); "the rudiments of his education. . . . The kindergarten period lasted until Billy was ten; . . . graduated him to a higher grade, so that at twelve he was robbing. . . ." (7); "a determination to learn to handle his mitts scientifically . . . he picked up pugilistic lore . . . along with the rudiments and finer points of its science. . . ." (8); "he had acquired an enviable knowledge of the manly art of self-defense" (12); "this was to hasten Billy's nautical education. . . ." (19), etc.

15. Lupoff, *Edgar Rice Burroughs,* 281.

16. Cf. also pages 75 ("the clean country"), 89 ("here in the country you can really *live.* You city people don't know what life is."), and 90 ("Nobody who has simply survived the counterfeit life of the city knows anything about living. You wait—we'll show you!").

17. But not all! Burroughs here goes to some length to dispel popular conceptions about the universal savagery and cruelty of the Apaches. Thus, while he never conceals their cruelty, nor is he hesitant to draw invidious comparisons with "civilized" practices: "they inflicted unspeakable torture upon the dying and nameless indignities upon the dead that would have filled with envy the high-minded Christian inquisitors of the sixteenth century" (51).

With this description, compare, for example, pages 37 ("he found no pleasure in inflicting pain upon the helpless; nor did this mark him particularly as different from his fellows, as there were others who shared his indifference to this form of sport. Apaches are human and as individuals of other human races vary in their characteristics, so Apaches vary. The Apaches were neither all good, nor all bad") and 89 ("when I see warriors torturing the helpless wounded and the defenseless prisoner, mutilating dead men who have fought bravely, something comes into my heart which is not pride of my people. I am ashamed, Ish-kay-nay, of even my own father, Geronimo.").

18. In fact the second novel, *The Apache Devil,* was written in the following year (1927).

19. For example, the character named Lieutenant King, who is portrayed as a model military man (graduate of West Point), may well be a private nod by Burroughs in recognition of his instructor, Captain Charles King (himself a graduate of West Point [1866]), at the Michigan Military Academy some thirty-odd years earlier, a man whom he admired enormously ("a man who has been an inspiration to me all my life because of his outstanding qualities as a soldier, a cavalryman and a friend" [see *ERB,* 95, 610f. and passim]).

Chapter Six

1. It has seemed best in the present volume to disregard, with one exception (the work of Michael Orth in *ERB-dom* volumes 81–86 [1975–76]), the sometimes uncritical panegyrics of the master that have appeared in the various fanzines devoted to Burroughs and his works. The interested reader will, however, find much of value scattered throughout the pages of such organs as *Edgar Rice Burroughs Quarterly* (only one issue published), *The Burroughs Bulletin, Erbania, ERB-dom* (no longer in publication), and *The Gridley Wave.*

2. For example, Gore Vidal, "Tarzan Revisited," *Esquire* 60 (December 1963): 192–93, 262, 264; and Robert E. Morsberger, "Edgar Rice Burroughs' Apache Epic," *Journal of Popular Culture* 7 (1973): 280–87.

3. For example, Ron Goulart *Cheap Thrills: An Informal History of the Pulp Magazines* (New Rochelle, 1972), chap. 10 ("Tarzan and the Barbarians"); and Kingsley Amis, *New Maps of Hell: A Survey of Science Fiction* (New York, 1960), 45–46, 65.

4. I intentionally omit from detailed discussion the study by Fenton, *The Big Swingers,* (Englewood Cliffs, 1967); the specialized *Tarzan of the Movies* by Gabe Essoe (New York, 1968); the work in French by Francis Lacassin, *Tarzan, ou le Chevalier Crispé* (Paris, 1971); and the volume by Philip Jose Farmer entitled *Tarzan Alive* (Garden City, 1972). The work by Fenton contains much unreliable information, and such bibliographic detail as it offers is now largely dated by the scholarly biography of Irwin Porges. Essoe's work, though quite intriguing in its own right, deals, as the title indicates, not with the literary Tarzan of Burroughs but with the cinematic travesty concocted by generations of meretricious Hollywood hacks; the book contains many still photos from the various movies, and offers a fairly detailed history of screen adaptations of the apeman. Lacassin's work is unlikely to appeal to English-speaking readers, but is not without interest for the dedicated Burroughs fan; Lacassin's emphasis is not so much the literary output as it is the movies and comics, in which Tarzan gained a kind of second (and often quite variant) personality. Farmer's book, though clever and ingenious, is a "reconstruction" of Lord Greystoke's lineage and an attempt to connect him with various other notables of popular literature, including Sherlock Holmes; it thus has little direct bearing on the present enterprise.

5. In Lupoff, *Edgar Rice Burroughs,* (New York, 1968).

6. Lupoff, *Barsoom,* (Baltimore, 1976). Only 1500 copies of this work were printed, and hence it is now difficult to find.

7. *Sleuthing in the Stacks,* (Cambridge, Mass.: Harvard University Press, 1944).

8. Robert E. Morsberger, "Edgar Rice Burroughs' Apache Epics," *Journal of Popular Culture* 7, no. 2 (Fall, 1973): 280–87.

9. Gary Topping, "The Pastoral Ideal in Popular American Literature: Zane Grey and Edgar Rice Burroughs," *Rendezvous: Idaho State University Journal of Arts and Letters* 12, no. 2 (Fall, 1977): 11–25.

Selected Bibliography

PRIMARY SOURCES

1. Mars Series
A Princess of Mars. 1912. Reprint. New York: Random House, Ballantine
    Books, 1981.
The Gods of Mars. 1913. Reprint. New York: Random House, Ballantine
    Books, 1981.
The Warlord of Mars. 1913. Reprint. New York: Random House, Bal-
    lantine Books, 1981.
Thuvia, Maid of Mars. 1916. Reprint. New York: Random House, Bal-
    lantine Books, 1981.
The Chessmen of Mars. 1922. Reprint. New York: Random House, Bal-
    lantine Books, 1981.
The Mastermind of Mars. 1927. Reprint. New York: Random House,
    Ballantine Books, 1982.
A Fighting Man of Mars. 1930. Reprint. New York: Random House,
    Ballantine Books, 1981.
Swords of Mars. 1934, 1935. Reprint. New York: Random House, Bal-
    lantine Books, 1980.
Synthetic Men of Mars. 1938, 1939. Reprint. New York: Random House,
    Ballantine Books, 1981
Llana of Gathol. 1941. Reprint. New York: Random House, Ballantine
    Books, 1981.
John Carter of Mars. 1940, 1942. Reprint. New York: Random House,
    Ballantine Books, 1981.

2. Pellucidar Series
At The Earth's Core. 1914. Reprint. New York: Grosset & Dunlap, Ace
    Books [no date].
Pellucidar. 1915. Reprint. New York: Grosset & Dunlap, Ace Books,
    1982.
Tanar of Pellucidar. 1929. Reprint. New York: Grosset & Dunlap, Ace
    Books, 1973.
Back to the Stone Age. 1936. Reprint. New York: Grosset & Dunlap, Ace
    Books [no date].
Land of Terror. 1944. Reprint. New York: Charter Communications, Ace
    Books [no date].

Savage Pellucidar. 1941, 1942, 1963. Reprint. New York: Grosset & Dunlap, Ace Books [no date].

3. Tarzan Series

Tarzan of the Apes. 1912, 1939. Reprint. New York: Random House, Ballantine Books, 1963.

The Return of Tarzan. 1913, 1941. Reprint. New York: Random House, Ballantine Books, 1963.

The Beasts of Tarzan. 1914. Reprint. New York: Random House, Ballantine Books, 1963.

The Son of Tarzan. 1915, 1916. Reprint. New York: Random House, Ballantine Books, 1963.

Tarzan and the Jewels of Opar. 1916. Reprint. New York: Random House, Ballantine Books, 1963.

Jungle Tales of Tarzan. 1916, 1917. Reprint. New York: Random House, Ballantine Books, 1963.

Tarzan the Untamed. 1919, 1920. Reprint. New York: Random House, Ballantine Books, 1963.

Tarzan the Terrible. 1921. Reprint. New York: Random House, Ballantine Books, 1963.

Tarzan and the Golden Lion. 1922, 1923. Reprint. New York: Random House, Ballantine Books, 1963.

Tarzan and the Ant Men. 1924. Reprint. New York: Random House, Ballantine Books, 1963.

Tarzan Lord of the Jungle. 1927, 1928. Reprint. New York: Random House, Ballantine Books, 1963.

Tarzan and the Lost Empire. 1928, 1929. Reprint. New York: Random House, Ballantine Books, 1963.

Tarzan at the Earth's Core. 1930. Reprint. New York: Random House, Ballantine Books, 1964.

Tarzan the Invincible. 1931. Reprint. New York: Random House, Ballantine Books, 1964.

Tarzan Triumphant. 1932. Reprint. New York: Random House, Ballantine Books, 1964.

Tarzan and the City of Gold. 1933. Reprint. New York: Random House, Ballantine Books, 1964.

Tarzan and the Lion Man. 1934. Reprint. New York: Random House, Ballantine Books, 1964.

Tarzan and the Leopard Men. 1935. Reprint. New York: Random House, Ballantine Books, 1964.

Tarzan's Quest. 1935, 1936. Reprint. New York: Random House, Ballantine Books, 1964.

Tarzan and the Forbidden City. 1938, 1941, 1966. Reprint. New York: Random House, Ballantine Books, 1964.

Tarzan the Magnificent. 1936, 1937, 1938, 1939, 1964, 1965, 1966, 1967. Reprint. New York: Random House, Ballantine Books, 1964.

Tarzan and the Foreign Legion. 1947. Reprint. New York: Random House, Ballantine Books, 1964.

Tarzan and the Madman. 1964. Reprint. New York: Random House, Ballantine Books, 1965.

Tarzan and the Castaways. 1940, 1941, 1964. Reprint. New York: Random House, Ballantine Books, 1965.

4. Venus Series

Pirates of Venus. 1932. Reprint. New York: Grosset & Dunlap, Ace Books, 1979.

Lost on Venus. 1933. Reprint. New York: Grosset & Dunlap, Ace Books, 1979.

Carson of Venus. 1938. Reprint. New York: Grosset & Dunlap, Ace Books, 1979.

Escape on Venus. 1946. Reprint. New York: Grosset & Dunlap, Ace Books, 1979.

The Wizard of Venus. 1964. Reprint. New York: Grosset & Dunlap, Ace Books, 1979.

5. Miscellaneous Works (in alphabetical order)

Apache Devil. 1933. Reprint. New York: Random House, Ballantine Books, 1964.

Beyond the Farthest Star. 1964. Reprint. New York: Charter Communications, Ace Books, 1973.

I Am a Barbarian. New York: Grosset & Dunlap, Ace Books, 1967.

Pirate Blood. 1970. (Also contains *The Wizard of Venus*). Reprint. New York: Grosset & Dunlap, Ace Books [no date].

The Bandit of Hell's Bend. 1924, 1952. Reprint. New York: Grosset & Dunlap, Ace Books [no date].

The Cave Girl. 1913, 1941. (Also contains "The Cave Man" [1963]). Reprint. New York: Grosset & Dunlap, Ace Books [no date].

The Deputy Sheriff of Commanche County. 1940. Reprint. New York: Charter Communications, Ace Books, 1979.

The Efficiency Expert. 1921, 1966, 1976. Reprint. *The Burroughs Bulletin,* nos. 57-58. Kansas City: The Burroughs Bibliophile, 1976.

The Eternal Lover. N.p.: A. C. McClurg & Co., 1925.

The Girl from Farris's. 1916, 1956. Reprint. New York: Grosset & Dunlap, Ace Books, 1979.

The Girl from Hollywood. 1922, 1950. Reprint. New York: Grosset & Dunlap, Ace Books [no date].

The Jungle Girl. Edgar Rice Burroughs, 1932.
The Lad and the Lion. 1917, 1938. Reprint. New York: Grosset & Dunlap, Ace Books [no date].
The Land that Time Forgot. N.p.: A. C. McClurg & Co., 1924.
The Mad King. 1914. Reprint. New York: Grosset & Dunlap, Ace Books [no date].
The Monster Men. 1929. Reprint. N.p.: Canaveral Press [no date].
The Moon Maid. 1923. Reprint. New York: Grosset & Dunlap, Ace Books [no date].
The Moon Men. 1925. Reprint. New York: Charter Communications, Ace Books [no date].
The Mucker. 1914. Reprint. New York: Charter Communications, Ace Books, 1974.
The Oakdale Affair and the Rider. 1937. Reprint. New York: Grosset & Dunlap, Ace Books, 1979.
The Outlaw of Torn. 1914. Reprint. New York: Grosset & Dunlap, Ace Books [no date].
The People that Time Forgot. 1918. Reprint. New York: Grosset & Dunlap, Ace Books, 1981.
The Red Hawk. 1925. Reprint. New York: Charter Communications, Ace Books [no date].
The Resurrection of Jimber-Jaw. *Argosy* (20 February 1937).
The War Chief. 1964. Reprint. New York: Random House, Ballantine Books, 1975.

SECONDARY SOURCES

1. Journal Articles

Flautz, John T. "An American Demagogue in Barsoom." *Journal of Popular Culture* 1 (1967): 263–75.
Hart, Irving Harlow. "The Most Popular Authors of Fiction in the Post-War Period, 1919–1926." *Publishers' Weekly* 111 (12 March 1927): 1045–53.
———. "The One Hundred Leading Authors of Best Sellers in Fiction from 1895 to 1944." *Publishers' Weekly* 149 (19 January 1946): 285–90.
Holtsmark, Erling B. "Spiritual Rebirth of the Hero: *Odyssey* 5," *Classical Journal* 61, no. 5 (February 1966): 206–7.
Mandel, Paul. "Tarzan of the Paperbacks." *Life* 55, no. 22 (29 November 1963): 11–12.
Morsberger, Robert E. "Edgar Rice Burroughs' Apache Epic." *Journal of Popular Culture* 7 (1973): 280–87.

Mullen, Richard D. "Edgar Rice Burroughs and the Fate Worse Than Death."*Riverside Quarterly* 4 (June 1970): 187ff.

Orth, Michael. "The Vaults of Opar, or Through the American Mind with Camera, Gun and Knife." *ERB-dom* 81–86 (1975–76).

Slate, Tom. "ERB and the Heroic Epic." *Riverside Quarterly* 3 (March 1968): 118–23.

Topping, Gary. "The Pastoral Ideal in Popular American Literature: Zane Grey and Edgar Rice Burroughs." *Rendezvous: Idaho State University Journal of Arts and Letters* 12, no. 2 (1977): 11–25.

Vidal, Gore. "Tarzan Revisited." *Esquire* 60 (December 1963): 192–93, 262, 264.

2. Fanzines Specializing in Burroughs

Edgar Rice Burroughs Quarterly (now discontinued). George T. McWhorter, Editor, Department of Rare Books, University of Louisville Library, Louisville, Kentucky 40292.

Erbania. D. Peter Ogden, Editor, 8001 Fernview Lane, Tampa, Florida 33615.

ERB-dom (now discontinued). C. E. Cazedessus, Jr., Editor, P. O. Box 507, St. Francisville, Louisiana 70775.

The Burroughs Bulletin. Vernell Coriell, Editor, 1301 Ann Eliza Street, Pekin, Illinois 61554.

3. Books

Aldiss, Brian W. *Billion Year Spree: The True History of Science Fiction.* New York: Doubleday & Co., 1973.

Amis, Kingsley. *New Maps of Hell: A Survey of Science Fiction.* New York: Harcourt, Brace & Co., 1960.

Bleiler, E. F. *Eight Dime Novels.* New York: Dover Publications, 1974.

Bailey, J. O. *Pilgrims through Space and Time: Trends and Patterns in Scientific and Utopian Fiction.* New York: Argus Books, 1947.

Easton, Robert. *Max Brand: The Big "Westerner."* Norman: University of Oklahoma Press, 1970.

Essoe, Gabe. *Tarzan of the Movies.* 1968. 2d. ed. Secaucus: Citadel Press, 1973.

Farmer, Philip Jose. *Tarzan Alive.* Garden City: Doubleday & Co., 1972.

Fenton, Robert. J. *The Big Swingers.* Englewood Cliffs: Prentice-Hall, 1967.

Goodstone, Tony. *The Pulps: Fifty Years of American Pop Culture.* New York: Chelsea House, 1970.

Goulart, Ron. *Cheap Thrills: An Informal History of the Pulp Magazines.* New Rochelle: Arlington House, 1972.

Gruber, Frank. *The Pulp Jungle.* Los Angeles: Sherbourne Press, 1967.

128 EDGAR RICE BURROUGHS

Hackett, Alice Payne. *70 Years of Best Sellers 1895–1965.* New York: R. R. Bowker Co., 1967.

Hart, James D. *The Popular Book: A History of America's Literary Taste.* Berkeley: University of California Press, 1963.

Heins, Henry Hardy. *A Golden Anniversary Bibliography of Edgar Rice Burroughs.* West Kingston, R.I.: Donald M. Grant, 1964.

Henkin, Leo J. *Darwinism in the English Novel 1860–1910: The Impact of Evolution on Victorian Fiction.* New York: Corporate Press, 1940.

Holtsmark, Erling B. *Tarzan and Tradition: Classical Myth in Popular Literature.* Westport: Greenwood Press, 1981.

Hughes, Dorthy B. *Erle Stanley Gardner: The Case of the Real Perry Mason.* New York: William Morrow & Co., 1978.

Lacassin, Francis. *Tarzan, ou le Chevalier Crispé,* Paris: Christian Bourgois, 1971.

Leavis, Q. D. *Fiction and the Reading Public.* London: Chatto & Windus, 1932 [1965].

Lupoff, Richard A. *Edgar Rice Borroughs: Master of Adlventure.* Rev. ed. New York: Charter Communications, Ace Books, 1968.

———. *Barsoom: Edgar Rice Burroughs and the Martian Vision.* Baltimore: Mirage Press, 1976.

Moskowitz, Sam. *Explorers of the Infinite: Shapers of Science Fiction.* New York: World Publishing Co., 1963.

———, ed. *Under the Moons of Mars: A History and Anthology of "The Scientific Romance" in the Munsey Magazines, 1912–1920.* New York: Hold, Rinehart & Winston, 1970.

Mott, Frank Luther. *Golden Multitudes: The Story of Best Sellers in the United States.* New York: Macmillan Co., 1947.

Porges, Irwin. *Edgar Rice Borroughs: The Man Who Created Tarzan.* Provo: Brigham Young University Press, 1975.

Richardson, Darrell C. *Max Brand: The Man and his Work.* Los Angeles: Fantasy Publishing Co., 1952.

Roy, John Flint. *A Guide to Barsoom: The Mars of Edgar Rice Burroughs.* New York: Ballatine Books, 1976.

Rush, N. Owen. *The Diversions of a Westerner: With Emphasis upon Owen Wister and Frederic Remington.* Amarillo: Books and Libraries, 1979.

Street, Brian V. *The Savage in Literature: Representations of "Primitive" Society in English Fiction 1858–1920.* London: Routledge & Kegan Paul, 1975.

Index

Abner Perry, 76, 77, 78, 79, 82
Abraham, 44, 59
Achilles, 53, 54, 64
Aeneas, 18, 22, 23, 29, 54, 84, 85, 91, 113n8
Alcmene, 54
alcohol, 12, 45, 47
Aldiss, Brian, 82, 105
Alger, Horatio, 71
Alice Rutherford, 53, 59, 63
All-Story, 6, 7, 71
All-Story Cavalier, 8
Altrochi, Rudolph, 99
Amazons, 83, 89
Ambler, Eric, 58
Amis, Kingsley, 104
Anchises, 54
Andy MacDuff, 95
Angustus the Ephesian, 43–44
Apaches, 3, 18, 19, 37, 38, 95–97, 106, 120n17
Aphrodite, 54
Apollo, 35
Arabs, 61, 107
Archimedes Q. Porter, 65
Argosy, 5, 71
Aristophanes, 23, 49
Aristotle, 48
Arizona, 3, 9, 18, 19, 37
Arnold, Edwin Lester, 99
Astok, 29–30
Australia, 14

Bailey, J. O., 104
Barbara Collis, 44, 45, 47, 61
Barbara Harding, 93
Barclay, Florence, 68, 69
Bellerophon, 53
Belthar, 67
Betty Caldwell, 89
bildungsroman, 49, 65, 93
Billings, 59
Billy Byrne, 93
Brand, Max, 72, 118n26
Bubonovitch, 36
Buchanan, Lord, 72

Bukawai, 42
Burroughs, Edgar Rice, attitude toward Indians, 37, 95–97; attitude toward race relations, 45–46, 48, 102–3, 104, 109, 115n16; attitude toward women, 48, 81; birthplace, 1; brothers, 1–2; business ventures, 3, 4–5, 6, 8, 11; childhood, 2; children, 5, 7, 9, 10, 13; columnist, 13; critique of writing, *107–10;* dealings with editors, 6, 7–8, 10, 101; divorce, 12, 14, 80; drinking problems, 12–13; father, 4; Hollywood dealings, 8, 10, 12, 94; illnesses, 11, 14, 15; influences on, 1, 34, 35, 38–39, 71, 99, 101, 114n4; intensity of writing, 8, 10, 12, 15, 107; interest in animals, 2, 12; jobs, 4; literary success, 6, 9–10, 68, 72; marriage, 4, 12, 14; military involvement, 3, 4, 8–9, 13; parents, 1, 62; patriotism, 9, 61; Pearl Harbor, 13; pessimism, 58–59, 61; pilot, 12; politics, 14, 42, 60–61; popularity, 11, 16, 33, 67–70, 98, 104, 107; populism, 7, 14; prejudices, 9, 13, 48–49; pseudonym, 6; religious views, 15, 41, 43, 44–45; research, 38; restlessness, 3, 4; sales of writings, 5–6, 7–8, 10, 68, 73; schooling, 2–3, 35, 62, 101, 103; sense of humor, 23, 31, 39, 103; shortcomings as writer, 30–31, 32, 81, 84, 85–86, 87, 90–91, 100, 108; social awareness, 24, 46, 48–49, 76, 77, 79, 92, 93, 96; speculations, 31–32; teaching career, 3; traditionalist, 20, 54; translations of books, 9, 11; travels, 7, 8, 9; use of language, 22, 73, 93, 103, 107, 113n9, 114n13, 119n7; war correspondent, 9, 14; wives: see Hulbert, Emma, and Dearholt, Florence.

WORKS:
At the Earth's Core, 76, 78
Apache Devil, The, 37, 95
Back to the Stone Age, 76
Beasts of Tarzan, The, 7, 64, 65
Carson of Venus, 82, 83, 84, 88, 89, 90
Cave Girl, The, 7, 8
Cave Man, The, 8

129